S

On Being a Workaholic
by Harris Kern

© Copyright 2015 by Harris Kern

ISBN 978-1-63393-092-6

Published by

 köehlerbooks™

210 60th Street
Virginia Beach, VA 23451
212-574-7939
www.koehlerbooks.com

ON BEING A WORK AHOLIC

USING BALANCE AND DISCIPLINE TO LIVE A BETTER AND MORE EFFICIENT LIFE

HARRIS KERN

VIRGINIA BEACH
CAPE CHARLES

S

TABLE OF CONTENTS

ON BEING A WORKAHOLIC

DEDICATION

I dedicate this book to my wife Mayra and my children (Chade, Kevin, CJ and Christian) whom I love very much and who provide me with great joy and fulfillment. It is also dedicated to Leticia Gomez, a special friend and business associate who has saved me from the pit of despair and loneliness on several occasions. You are truly an Earth Angel!

INTRODUCTION

Admittedly, there has been a sundry of books written and published about workaholics that teaches them how to deal with their problematic and oftentimes unhealthy lifestyles. The trouble is that most of these books have failed to resonate with readers on a more personal level because the majority of them have been authored by psychologists and psychiatrists. This book, however, is penned by the ultimate workaholic, who goes by the name of Harris Kern, Yours Truly.

Technically, you can't really classify me as a workaholic. I actually exceeded that label about three decades ago. I'm as extreme as they come. For most of my life, I've really pushed the envelope by taking my rigorous exercise routine and career with its myriad of accomplishments to a whole different level. People who know me well have often said I am robotlike in everything I do. In retrospect, it would be rather pointless for me to attempt to defy that claim. Doing so would be like trying to cover the sun with my pinkie finger.

After giving it a great deal of thought, I decided to tackle this subject head-on because I've learned the hard way that being a workaholic is dangerous. It's become a serious epidemic. By my definition, a workaholic is someone who puts all their eggs (resources) into one or two baskets and focuses solely on one or two priorities. Most make it one priority, their career. However, some actually dedicate 100 percent of their efforts into other priorities like their health or their relationships. Then there are those stubborn ones who have a total disregard for relationships and only concentrate on two of the three big priorities in life, just like I did. Forsaking everyone who cared about me, I focused on my career and health. Needless to say, I aced them both. But the biggest mistake I made in my life is that I left one very important priority out of this equation—*relationships*. I put my family and spirituality on the backburner for so long that in the end it cost me dearly.

A Cautionary Tale Straight from the Horse's Mouth

Believe me when I say focusing on one or two priorities will eventually catch up with you and take you down. I learned this the hard way. I thought that focusing solely on two out of these three priorities would be the right way to live my life because it would make me successful and healthy. That in the end the people I cared about would benefit from my success. Although friends and colleagues warned me to slow down and enjoy time with my beautiful family, I simply wouldn't hear of it.

I was the ultimate workaholic—an unstoppable machine. Nothing or no one could break my resolve or focus. In time, I completely lost sight of what mattered most in my life. I abandoned my morals. My conscience had become so seared that I broke a few serious commandments. I also thought that balance was overrated, an overused word. The concept of living a balanced lifestyle and being successful seemed like an oxymoron to me. I felt that it wasn't realistic. Something had to give if I was to continue my path to success. The easiest thing to sacrifice was my family and spirituality.

Instead of taking care of my relationships, I focused on money, power, physique, excitement and sex. The life I led had all the makings of a great movie. Heck, it might have even been a box-office hit. Unfortunately, this movie nearly had a tragic ending. The main character almost killed himself. But instead of taking the easy way out, I fought back and with some help from a few special people. I lived through the darkest time in my life to write this book.

Back when I was in a very bad place, death would have surely been the easiest way out for me. At the age of 60, I found myself confronting my biggest fear of all—being alone. Up until this point in my life, I had never lived alone. But there I was, living in a spacious five-thousand-square-foot home with six empty bedrooms and no friends or family around me. I was living in a suburb north of Dallas, Texas, and didn't really know anyone except my real estate agent—who has become a good friend. I kept too busy to socialize with others. As a defense mechanism against my loneliness, I worked long hours and exercised seven days a week (like always)—whatever it took to mask the pain. But now I have taken a 360-degree turn by introducing spirituality back into my life. Sure, I still have days when the only thing that keeps me going is the memories I have of my wife and children. But my renewed faith and outlook on life is what sustains me day by day.

Presently, my biggest goal is to have my family return to my life. I hope that with God's help and guidance, that will happen. For now all I can do is keep praying and adhere to the morals I should have adopted way back then, which are now front and center every day. My plight is truly a remarkable story and it is my hope that it will help all workaholics who read this book come to their senses before it's too late. Here are a few key points about this book that I'd like you, the reader, to keep in mind:

- This is not merely another self-help book—it's an investigative and brutally honest look into the lives of workaholics.
- The book has been structured into five major sections as highlighted in the graphics below.
- It features a simplified three-step process that will teach you how to first institute balance into your life and then maintain that balance.

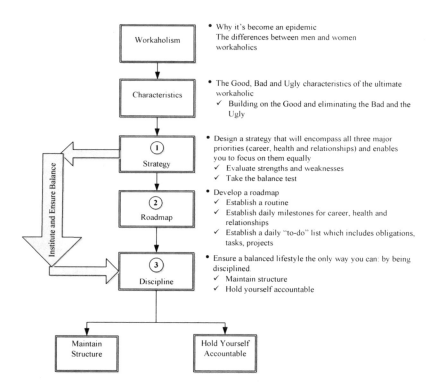

Below are the five key sections of the book explained in more detail:

1. Why is *workaholism* such an epidemic all over the world? It's not only in the United States. Global economies have become more competitive. As an employee you will have no choice but to be more productive with fewer resources.

2. Identify the good, bad and ugly *characteristics* of the ultimate workaholic. There are some good traits to being a workaholic, but unfortunately the bad and ugly ones always trump the good ones. Unless, you recognize those nasty ones and proactively deal with them, those negative traits will eventually catch up to your daily lifestyle and you will take that hard fall—guaranteed.

3. It starts with a thorough evaluation to understand your strengths and weaknesses, then taking the balance test. Know exactly where you stand. Once you do, then design

a *strategy* for living a happier and more productive life. It should include faith and focusing on your career, health and relationships equally.

4. Develop a *roadmap*. The roadmap should include a new daily routine encompassing all three priorities and focusing on your projects, tasks and obligations via a to-do list.

5. Be *disciplined* by maintaining structure (being organized, adhering to your routine and to-do list) and training your mind to hold yourself accountable. Honing your self-discipline skills is the key to maintaining a balanced, successful, thriving and happier life.

Interspersed throughout the book are true stories of my life as a longtime workaholic. If a die-hard workaholic and stubborn old man like me can turn my life around, then maybe there's hope that other people can be proactive and change direction before it's too late.

Chances are you never heard of me before buying this book. But after reading this, you just may be amazed at how successful and accomplished I was only to lose it all, then gain it back. It is my endeavor to help and inspire you to reach your full potential... regardless of your past circumstances... and whatever your goals.

CHAPTER ONE

Workaholism—A Widespread Epidemic

The escalating pressures of working tirelessly to put food on the table has taken a physical and emotional toll on many people. Succumbing to workaholism has destroyed relationships and families beyond repair. Many individuals have had premature life-shattering strokes or, worse yet, dropped dead of a heart attack because they focused solely on work, 24 hours a day, seven days a week, and rarely slowed down to relax and recharge their batteries. Most of these die-hard workaholics never exercised to maintain a good healthy lifestyle and they've had to pay the piper big-time for neglecting this important aspect of their lives.

Most people these days become workaholics out of sheer necessity. Unfortunately, world economies and cultures now dictate our working paradox like never before. Employers expect and demand their employees to be more productive with less resources. Mostly due to lackluster global economies, the working class is being forced to comply with these unreasonable demands and expectations, which puts them only one step above indentured servitude. No respectable working man or woman wants to risk losing their job and, let's face it, working a measly

40-hour work is a surefire way to put their livelihoods in jeopardy anytime there is a RIF.

It seems as though top-level management the world over aspires to hire individuals who are willing to eat and breathe their jobs, 365 days out of the year, and with little or no vacation time to speak of. Although it's illegal for management to actually come out and say this openly, they're constantly thinking it and finding discreet ways to enforce these unwritten work policies on unsuspecting employees. If layoffs can't be avoided and must be executed, typically those who are most productive and work the longest hours are the ones who are able to avoid "getting the axe." They have been on management's radar screen as superior performers.

Some people become workaholics because growing up they were reared to work hard by one or both of their parents. As a child, I was continuously told by my father and mother, "Harris, if you work hard in life, you will be rewarded with success." In retrospect, I was reminded a bit too much and eventually, I became obsessed. I turned into a relentless workaholic. He also said, "And let me remind you that your free ride is over—you need to start helping with household expenses." But this type of mentoring had its positive side. Many of my old friends from high school who weren't raised in this manner ended up being broke losers who always seemed to be down on their luck. Most of them got hooked on drugs, ended up incarcerated or got stuck in low-paying jobs and always struggled to pay their bills.

As crazy as it may seem, some individuals simply love the label of being a workaholic. Take me for instance. I always took great pride in my workaholic label. Every chance I got, I bragged about my work-related accomplishments to anyone who would listen. The more work that was thrown in my face, the more exhilarating life seemed to me. We now live in an extremely challenging world and I love to be put to the test constantly. For me this kind of hard-core scrutiny has always been rewarding, even after I went through a painful divorce with my first wife. I didn't learn my lesson and still gravitated right back to what I loved doing the most. It was my security blanket and the ultimate high. Good luck trying to get me to change my way of thinking and living—many had tried. Even now in my older years, I don't let up for a minute.

But I have learned to be more balanced by focusing more efforts into other key areas of my life.

There are individuals who are self-made workaholics. They were not born this way nor did they intend to become addicted to work. Their flawed personalities and perceptions of life coupled with a strong inclination toward addictive things have turned them into workaholics of the worst kind. These people thrive on work so much that, in time, they simply are not able to exist or function normally without it.

The harder I focused on work, the more accomplished it made me feel. Eventually that euphoria became my drug, one I simply could not live without. Pretty soon a few accomplishments will no longer fuel the addictive beast that you've become and, make no mistake, you will crave more and more triumphs and successes, enough to make your blood rise to the most elevated temperature you can stand.

As I type day in and day out on my computer trying to finish another book, I can still feel the excitement thinking about all of my past accomplishments. For me, life has always been all about accomplishments. My philosophy will never change. Without accomplishments, you merely exist; with accomplishments, you live life to the fullest. The trick here is to not work yourself to an early grave. My name is Harris Kern and I am a workaholic. I'm here to tell you that integrating relationships and health into your workaholic life to achieve balance and maintaining it with self-discipline could very well be your salvation. It certainly saved and redeemed this ultimate workaholic.

Work Habits Around the World

Working hard and long hours is not only prevalent in the United States. It is the norm in many countries like Japan, where it's an integrated part of the culture there. Many employees sacrifice their home life to work long hours to show their dedication to the company and hopefully be recognized in terms of salary and stature at the appropriate time. Being successful in one's career in Asia typically means many long evenings and weekends of work.

Such success is purely a status symbol. Odds are the harder you work, the more successful you become. Workaholism is highly respected by Japanese family members, especially spouses. It is unheard of to divorce someone because he or she is a workaholic as is done on a regular basis here in the United States.

Contrary to popular belief, not all Asians are hardworking, so I don't want to generalize. I have always thought it is quite unfair to stereotype a group of people. However, the main difference is that there it is widely accepted, while in the States it is called an "infectious disease."

Being addicted to work in Japan can actually be traced back centuries and it equates to success as it does in the United States. In reality, workaholism is a giant killer in Japan and is commonly referred to as *karoshi,* which translates to "death by overwork." Sadly, it is believed to cause more than 1,000 deaths a year: nearly 5 percent of the country's stroke and heart attack deaths in employees under age 60 can be attributed to workaholism. This rather unhealthy "state of being" seems to be in full bloom the world over. Here are the top five most workaholic countries, according to the Organization for Economic Co-operation and Development (OECD) and a 2014 article by Selena Maranjian:

1. Turkey has 46.13% of its employees working extremely long hours.
2. Japan has an estimated 31.7% of its workforce laboring long, extensive hours.
3. In Mexico, 28.63% of the population punches in the time clock way more than they should.
4. South Korea has an estimated 27.66% of its entire population working way beyond a forty-hour week.
5. In Israel, 17.58% of the workforce puts in regular overtime hours.

Employers Milking Employees

In harsh economic times, management always expects more mileage from their employees. The ugly truth is they have you right where they want you—scared and vulnerable. In the minds of top-level executives, they have a legitimate excuse to demand more, reduce their headcount, and constantly push their subordinates to the brink of physical and emotional exhaustion. But surprisingly, everyone who wants to keep getting a paycheck understands and complies without rattling any cages. Sure they may complain in secret, but the bottom line is they will continue to perform to the best of their ability and blame their predicament on the economy. In other words, they absolve management of its sins and go right on putting in extra hours for the same pay.

The employees who want nothing more than to survive *the cut* will do whatever it takes to keep their job. When cornered into this kind of situation, what should a relentless workaholic do? Years ago when I was faced with this kind of scenario, I took things to a whole different level. To make an impression, I brought a cot, sleeping bag, and extra clothes with me to my office with the intention of working many late nights. I usually worked until I fell asleep. Thank goodness my office building had decent showers. Despite getting very little sleep, I would still wake up at 4:30 A.M. and get to the gym, which opened at 5 A.M. I know this all sounds crazy, but keep in mind that I lived through some pretty ugly recessions in my four-plus decades in the corporate world. This extreme *modus operandi* of mine is the only way I was able to survive.

When the economy eventually does turn around, logic dictates that one would expect management to hire additional resources and hopefully demand less from their existing staff. At this juncture, most employees want their normal life back. Who can blame them? Most of them have probably reached their breaking point by then. Unfortunately, life isn't fair and things don't always work out in favor of the working class. Even after a recession is officially declared as being over, most companies ignore the change in times and continue to squeeze all the milk they can get from employees. Doing more with fewer resources is definitely a business model that is here to stay. Knowing that employees can be pushed to their breaking points without ramifications is quite a luxury for management these days. The odds are clearly in their favor.

Don't Wait for a Crisis to Happen

Sooner or later, your irresistible addiction to work will become a matter of life and death. It will happen—guaranteed. What goes up *will* eventually come down. Being oblivious to just about everything and everyone around you except your career *will* take you down. Forgetting about your morals will also eventually catch up to you. There's a reason why that old saying, *what goes around comes around,* has withstood the test of time. Ignoring all the people who care about you except those individuals you *use* to help further your career is oh so wrong. This is the most idiotic thing you can do.

There are many ups and downs in life. If you're not proactive by focusing on your relationships, health and career equally, you are destined for an emergency crash landing with little to no chance of survival. So before you go down that path to self-destruction, listen to someone who has been there more times than he'd care to admit. Don't wait for a crisis to happen to do something about your unhealthy work habits. Stop ignoring the other critical areas of your life before it's too late for redemption.

How Did You Become a Workaholic?

Many of my work-related mannerisms had everything to do with my upbringing. My father and mother worked extremely long hours to put a decent roof over our heads and food on the table. As an impressionable young man, I witnessed their efforts day in and day out. One day it hit me like a ton of bricks that having observed my parents work tirelessly to provide for our family had actually worn off on me. But the extremist in me took the strong work ethic that had been instilled in me to a whole new level. The main difference was that although my parents worked hard, they never forgot that family always came first. They always kept their priorities and morals in check.

Have you ever stopped to think how you or someone you're close to became a workaholic? What is it exactly that turned you or your loved one into a well-oiled machine, always eager and available to work around the clock? What are the factors that have driven you and others to *only* think about work day and night, as if nothing else exists in this world? Ask yourself the following soul searching questions:

- Have you become a workaholic because you weren't physically gifted in school and were constantly being bullied?
- Were you unpopular or considered to be a nerd by others during your teen years? Did this make you want to climb the corporate ladder just so you could prove to be more powerful than those who once mocked and made fun of you?
- Did you become addicted to work because you were afraid of being overlooked for promotions? Is this why you always

made a conscious effort to be the first to arrive and the last to leave the office?

- Have you always put work above everything else in your life because of the stiff competition you face on the job?
- Has work become your number one priority because down deep inside your lack of experience makes you feel insecure about your job?
- Do you tend to work harder and longer hours to make up for the fact that you never got a college degree?
- Does getting a hefty paycheck every two weeks make you crave more and more work?
- Did growing up under deprived circumstances turn you into the workaholic you are today?
- Do you work yourself to death so that your family won't have to suffer the same poverty you did growing up?

As a self-proclaimed workaholic, I can definitely relate to most of these questions. During my early teen years, a neighbor of mine who later became my mentor taught me how to be disciplined in every facet of life. He used to tell me repeatedly that living life is all about waking up every morning with a purpose and having many accomplishments. His motto when it came to life achievements was *the more, the better.*

Reflecting on the past, I've come to the realization that there were multiple reasons. I never paused to evaluate the way I was living my life until I took that hard fall from grace. I can't stress enough how important it is to fully explore the underlying reasons why you work as much as you do. If you ever feel you've reached your breaking point and decide to seek professional help, this information is going to be precisely what your counselor or doctor will need to come up with possible ways to treat your addiction to work.

Borne by Necessity

What choice does anyone have these days but to work more hours? Management in most companies keep piling on the demands with a total disregard for how this may affect home life for employees. It's all about the company's bottom line—its existence. This world is now filled with companies run by greedy executives who all seem to want and need to be more profitable at any cost.

As an employee, spouse, parent, etc., you place your own demands on yourself when it comes to family obligations, health-related goals, and other activities. Many people will tell you to work smarter, not harder. Obviously that goes without saying. Why wouldn't anyone in their right mind not opt to work as smart and efficiently as they possibly can? Other well-meaning individuals may advise you to maintain a balanced lifestyle. Again, this isn't exactly an innovative new concept. Who doesn't want to have a balanced lifestyle? Clearly, talk is cheap and easy to dish out. Considering that work responsibilities seem to keep multiplying for us faster than our own body's cells do, implementing changes that will allow you to live a balanced lifestyle almost seem impossible.

To complicate the matter even further, even your own company management will tell you one thing, but expect you to do the complete opposite. It's almost like they are employing reverse psychology on you. There may have been a time during your career that you were told something that sounds a lot like this, "You really should consider taking some time off" or "Don't sweat it. You can come in at 6 A.M. and not leave until 7 P.M." In the future, you may even hear the boss say, "You really do need to spend more time with your wife and kids." Granted, these are all honorable gestures and it sure would be nice to take them up on their kind offers without having to deal with any consequences. The naked truth is that while you are taking a much needed and well-deserved break, once you get back into the office there will be hell to pay with more work and aggressive deadlines.

When vacation time rolls around, you may also be told to enjoy your time off and avoid looking and responding to work emails while you're lying on the beach trying to get a suntan. However, at the same time, management itself continues to send you email after email, expecting you to respond, because business doesn't stop just because you're on vacation. Heaven forbid if you ever dare to take off early so that you can spend more time with your family. If you did this on a regular basis, do you honestly think your job will be safe? I'm willing to bet my last dollar that it won't be. There are way too many young single people who have no family obligations who need a good job. They've got the "eye of the tiger" and are willing to work around the clock to prove themselves. What choice do we have but to comply with work obligations on a dime? It's either dance to that tune or be fired.

Workaholic by Nature

Many people would categorize workaholics as introverts. Oftentimes, individuals who work nonstop are perceived by others to be more comfortable and secure in their work environment amongst business colleagues instead of socializing with friends at weddings, birthday parties, nightclubs, and other entertainment venues. However, I see things in a totally different light. In my opinion, most workaholics have excellent interpersonal skills and have been blessed with the gift of gab, but they are very selective as to who gets their time. They just don't see the return on investment (ROI) when it comes to spending time with people who do not have the clout to influence their career in a positive way. Sure, they may get together with friends occasionally, perhaps once a year, if that. However, they do see the value of socializing with their business colleagues to nurture key relationships for their personal advancement. It's in their DNA. Their personality revolves around the work they do. From a distance, you can see their face light up when discussing work activities. Sometimes you can almost see their minds drifting when talking about anything else. Nothing else in the world they live in matters, but their number one priority, work, excites them. They may not admit it openly, but their actions speak for them.

Natural workaholics hate to go on family vacations. They simply can't stand the idea of being taken away from their work environment or temporarily denied access to the technology that enables them to keep connected to their jobs. If it wasn't for the existence of handheld devices to check email and voicemail regularly, you can be sure that most natural workaholics would pull out their hair or worse suffer a mental breakdown. Their perception of an ideal vacation is getting up first thing in the morning to check their email, make whatever calls are necessary, and then *try* to have some fun with the family, in that order.

For the Love of Work

The most common and dangerous type of workaholic is someone who knows perfectly well he or she is a workaholic and they are proud of it. They are fully convinced that their lifestyle is the appropriate one for them and will even present the argument that their addiction to work benefits their family in the long-term. They have brainwashed themselves into thinking that their hard work and sacrifice will reap monetary rewards and outweigh any negatives. They may be right that all that hard work could benefit their family. Who in this day and age wouldn't benefit from having more income? However, will having a constant stream of money truly make up for all the long nights and weekends away from the family? Ask yourself: Who is kidding whom here? Don't be fooled, the long hours and constant focus on work, even when they're not at the office, clearly benefits the workaholic more than his or her loved ones. This lifestyle is heaven for the workaholic. It's the ultimate adrenalin rush they can't live without. It is the only true motivation they have to get out of bed in the morning. It's the engine that drives twenty-four hours a day, seven days a week.

Despite all of my trials and tribulations, I am still a workaholic and you can also label me a healthaholic because of the rigorous daily exercise routine I follow religiously. No matter what, I will never deviate from both of these things. In the end, I must stay true to myself. But through it all, I have learned to be more balanced by focusing on *relationships* and making them my third number one priority when they used to be right at the bottom of the totem pole. I was and always will be the *ultimate* workaholic. The only difference now is that my faith and family comes first in my life.

Before introducing *impactful relationships* into my life nothing else mattered. As a matter of fact, I used to tout that my priorities were *money, gym* and *sex*, all in that order. When my quota of money and gym time were met for the day, I rewarded myself with sex. For more than three decades, my life revolved around my career and exercise regimen. Sex was just icing on the cake, but there was no focus on building and nurturing personal relationships.

Happy workaholics don't think there's anything wrong with their lifestyle. Working long hours without a day off is no big deal to them. The reality is they can't get enough of work. The word "burnout" is simply not in their vocabulary. Slowing down is never an option. They figure that, like Weird Al Yankovic says, they'll be mellow when they're dead. The more they have going on in their workplace, the more thrilling it is. The more they accomplish, the happier they are. It's never enough because they are hardcore junkies. They will only consider slowing down when a crisis of some kind forces them to, like the prospect of losing their marriage or becoming seriously ill. Nine times out of ten, their mind is engulfed in work. Even when people are speaking to them about non-work-related things, they are rhetorically strategizing about their next steps back at the office. Since they don't want to be disrespectful, natural workaholics will typically tune into every third or fourth word another person is saying. They have become so good at this that they hide their inattention from friends and family, but really, work is the only thing that can hold their attention.

As for me, turning my computer on to check email first thing in the morning and then moving on to the myriad of projects I have planned for the day excites me more than a Victoria's Secret ad on television. This will never change. What I have learned to do though is figure out how to institute and maintain balance so I don't lose sight of my family and other things that are more important than work. Workaholics tend to put everything on the back burner—especially their spirituality. Once your consciousness allows you to do this, then neglecting your family's needs will easily follow. Dedicating a few minutes here and there to family and your spirituality will make you an unhappy workaholic in time.

A One-Track Mind

The happy workaholic's world revolves around one priority. Wouldn't life be so much easier if you *only* had one priority to worry about every day? Of course it would! Happy-go-lucky workaholics get up at the crack of dawn thinking about work. And they go to bed thinking about the same thing. They have a one-track mind and all they care about is their career. The more money they make, the better and happier they will be. The more they accomplish in their career, the bigger of a payoff they are destined to have. I lived most of my life being a slave to two priorities, which were excelling in my career and maintaining my health (diet and exercise). It was all about me and no one else. In my eyes, I had it all. I was healthy and in awesome shape with an ego the size of the Grand Canyon. I thought of myself as being invincible and of course I was that highly accomplished executive that could do no wrong. Totally oblivious to what others around me thought, I was a legend in my own mind. Little did I know how truly pathetic I was.

While I was solely focusing on making myself happy, my first wife managed the household and practically raised our daughter single-handedly. She also worked part-time. I did make it a point to play with my daughter and spoil her rotten, but I did it with an ulterior motive in mind. The trick was to keep her occupied and entertained so that I could do more. In other words, my objective was to fulfill my fatherly obligations so that I could get back to work as quickly as possible. Even when I designated time to play with my daughter, my mind and heart were always elsewhere. My mistake was that I failed to savor those moments with my daughter, which was clearly an act of stupidity on my part.

Not Accountable to Anyone Else

There I was living the good life, not only because I was the main bread-winner, but my job gave me the luxury of traveling the world and doing whatever I wanted, whenever I wanted. Sometimes I would even orchestrate unnecessary business trips and no one would ever get suspicious. I was on top of the world, eating my cake day and night, until it all finally caught up with me and the empire came crashing down on me.

I went from having the best of both worlds where my wife would take care of all household matters (except for the finances, as I trusted no one else when it came to money) to hitting rock bottom. But before that unforeseen occurrence, I pretty much had free reign to do whatever I needed to advance my career. No one, not even my wife, could question my decisions and actions. In retrospect one of my biggest achievements in life was being awarded my own Information Technology (IT) book imprint with Prentice Hall, one of the largest and most reputable publishers in the world. After having published dozens of books, it became easier to live a carefree lifestyle and never be accountable to anyone but myself.

Traveling all over the world, speaking before thousands of people and keeping up with my executive responsibilities was certainly a good life. In time, my name became synonymous with IT. My ego became so inflated that to this day I often wonder how I manage to fit into the many planes I flew in. Even though I seemed to have it all, I still wanted more. Young, beautiful women swarmed around me like flies. Needless to say, I did not have the self-discipline or willpower to resist the temptations. Since I was away from home base frequently, it was so easy for me to play the singles scene. So I did what many other executives have been known to do. Every time I boarded a plane, I discreetly took off my wedding ring and told myself, "What's the harm? No one will ever know." But I was dead wrong. As it turned out, God always had a front-row seat to the premiere showing of my life.

The fun continued for approximately a decade. I had girlfriends all over the world but it still wasn't enough. Lying became second nature to me. Not only did I lie to my wife, but I also deceived all the wonderful and honorable women I encountered along the way. To quench my never-ending thirst for sex, I used every pick-up line in the book to conquer each beauty and get to the Promised Land, which was usually between their legs. That was the extent of my spirituality. The goal was to get each one in bed. The more notches I had on my bed post, the manlier I felt. Some of these unsuspecting women actually became my girlfriends. There was always a girl waiting for me in every port.

The way I went from one woman to the next without giving it a second thought was rather pathetic. It was a disgusting way of treating the opposite sex. I wanted each girl to believe they were special and the only one in my life. Like a broken record, I lied over and over again just to satisfy my selfish needs. It was a blast at the time, a fun game that I never wanted to end. What I didn't know at the time or care to believe was that God was watching and keeping score all along. While I was leading a superficial life, He was depositing my bad deeds into an eternal bank to be withdrawn at the appropriate time.

When you're living the good life, you don't stop to reflect or apologize for all of your sins. The truth is you don't want to reflect on all the pain you've inflicted on others because you're on top of the world. Hey if it feels good, it must be good—right? I didn't want to believe my actions were really that bad. In my heart of hearts I knew they were bad, but in my mind. everything was justified to make myself look good.

Male and Female Workaholics

I never realized how much of a big difference there is between male and female workaholics until I took a close look at the way my business partner Leticia manages her day versus the way I do mine. Leticia loves her career and works hard at it, but she's not as addicted to work as yours truly is. She has two teenaged kids and a husband to take care of. As if that's not enough, she also wears several different hats in her professional world. Aside from running her own literary agency, Leticia is an acquisition editor for an independent Virginia-based publisher and more recently became the publisher of her very own book imprint.

To say that she has a full plate is an understatement, but somehow Leticia is able to maintain a balanced lifestyle, devoting ample time for her relationships, career, and family. She even finds the time to have meaningful conversations with her friends, clients, and business associates. My business partner's weakness is that she loves to babble. Her conversations take twice as long as they should. I estimate that on average she wastes approximately ten hours a week babbling. But that's what she loves to do. Leticia will argue that the constant babbling is a part of the formula that has made her successful. I have to admit that her gift of gab is critical to the initial sales process. After speaking with Leticia for the first time, prospective clients come away from the conversation feeling that she's sincere and trustworthy—which she is. There's no denying that her ability to talk to people is a huge reason she's been successful in the publishing industry. She genuinely cares about people and tries her best to make her clients happy. Furthermore, she's intelligent, extremely personable and genuine. Leticia is the total package.

In all fairness, I can't really compare Leticia to myself because it's like comparing apples to oranges. Her life is by far more challenging than mine. The question is: Does she manage it effectively? Nope! Actually, she does a horrible job of managing time, which in turn contributes to her feeling stressed out from the heavy workload, therefore making it seem like she really is a workaholic. Leticia needs to learn how to be a *nice asshole*—like me. She needs to become the kind of person who can say no more often. She also needs to learn how to cut off conversations earlier than she does and in the correct manner.

As for me, I am a true workaholic who works seven days a week. I am an addict to the nth degree. Typically, I work approximately seventy hours a week. I also wear different hats in my professional life. I am a full-time author, life coach, IT consultant, organization mentor, publisher of my own imprint, motivational speaker and I have a teenage daughter. I also exercise seven days a week. Managing my health is just as much a priority as my work. That is not the norm for most workaholics. They just work—period. Maintaining balance in all the areas of my life is now front and center for me. Now I make a conscientious effort to focus equally on the following three priorities: Relationships, Career and Health. Although Leticia works 40 to 50 hours a week, she has a demanding family to deal with as most career women do. Female workaholics are much more balanced than the typical male workaholic. The male workaholic puts their career first and foremost, while women never compromise their family obligations.

Workaholics and Hard Workers

A hard worker will diligently focus on his or her responsibilities during normal business hours. Once they leave the building or their home office their minds are no longer fixated on work. They punch out, leave work behind and start thinking about their personal life. Hard workers like what they do, are passionate about their job, and occasionally put in some long hours at the office. However, when they go home, their work stays at the office. They are physically and mentally at home with their family, friends or significant others. Their life doesn't revolve around the work they do. Following below are symptoms of individuals who really don't have any choice but to work around the clock.

- *Responsibility for a large family*: They have no choice but to work long hours because they are the main breadwinner. Usually they have many mouths to feed, bodies to clothe and have to maintain a home. These are the cards they've been dealt, so working hard and long hours is a way of life for them.
- *Migrant workers:* As immigrants they have come to this country to make a better life for themselves and their family. Typically they'll take whatever job they can get and at whatever measly salary their employer provides them with. In many instances, they will work multiple jobs to survive.

I do not consider these individuals to be certifiable workaholics. It is out of necessity that they work hard. To the "real deal" workaholic, nothing is or will ever be as satisfying as their job. Nothing is as exhilarating as completing that massive project ahead of schedule. The more projects they complete, the more accomplished they feel. Tackling tough challenges on a daily basis is what really turns them on. Their thrills come from work, not their personal life or other activities.

The workaholic is always motivated because they control their own destiny. They see their professional world as one happy team: "me, myself and I." In their personal world, they're not very successful because they are typically dealing with someone else they can't control or manipulate. The workaholic never leaves the building—you may see them physically exit their workplace, but mentally, they've never left. They never check out.

CHAPTER TWO

Flying in the Danger Zone

Believe it or not, there's much more to life than your career or business. To have a purpose-filled life, you also have to manage health and relationships, All three facets are equally important and each deserves the same attention or there will eventually be serious consequences to deal with. In this scenario, two out of three is bad, really bad. If you ignore your health and only focus on work, you can easily develop a serious health issue which could put you out of commission for a long time if not forever. On the flipside of the coin, if you ignore relationships and you're married, a divorce will be inevitable and that could bring you to your knees just as hard. Don't take things for granted, like I did. When you're on top of the world, like I was, and tuned out to everything around you except the things that can help you be ore successful, you will eventually pay a heavy price.

Please don't think of these predictions as idle threats. You would do well to heed the counsel of a man who turned his back on God, the woman he loved, family members and so many wonderful people. The question is: How can you prevent this from happening to you? What are the warning signs to look for? How can you become proactive and know when a crisis is about to happen? The first line of defense is to acknowledge that you have a problem.

Admitting You Have a Problem

When you're making tons of money, traveling the world over speaking in front of large audiences, treated like royalty and regarded as a foremost leading expert, why would anyone suspect something was wrong with the way you're living your life? It's rather difficult to put the brakes on and admit that there is a problem brewing when things are going that well for you. I focused so intensely on my career that it was constantly paying dividends. No wonder it took me over three decades to figure out that I had a problem, a really bad one.

In my twenties, thirties, and early forties it was all about my professional world. All that mattered to me was making plenty of money, being a great leader and becoming the top dog in the IT industry. Suffice it to say that it didn't come easy for me. I worked around the clock to make my name synonymous with IT. Of course, the money and power were gratifying. Although no one wants to admit it, this world revolves around money and I was always at the head of the line waiting to cash in on a bigger payday.

Am I a workaholic? Of course I am! I would be lying through my teeth if I said I wasn't one. Truthfully, being a workaholic is one of the things about myself that I'm most proud of. I don't need a psychiatrist to tell me that. In the past, when people referred to me as a workaholic, I simply shrugged it off by saying, "So what? Isn't that better than being lazy? Would I be better off going to bars and partying or sitting at home watching mind-numbing television?" For me, being a workaholic has been paying dividends for a long time. In fact I used to constantly joke with others about being a workaholic. Then I would look them in the eye and say, "Yes... all that hard work has made me successful." But eventually the day came when being an unstoppable workaholic backfired on me.

No matter how much wealth I accumulated or how far I climbed in my profession, it was never enough. I wanted to write more books, continue climbing to the top of the corporate world, and own several successful businesses. In time that kind of mentality cost me dearly, emotionally, physically and spiritually. I ended up going through an extremely painful divorce and, to make matters worse, I turned my back on God. Unfortunately, it took something of catastrophic proportions in my life to make me change my ways and put my faith first in my life for good.

Needless to say my downfall took me by complete surprise. Before that, I would always justify my long work weeks by bragging about how much money I was bringing home to the wife and kids. My rationale at the time was that I could make it up to my family by taking them on whirlwind vacations and buying elegant homes for them to live in. By my account, I was making my family the number one priority by giving them material things instead of my time. But I was dead wrong.

How Being a Workaholic Can Sabotage the Different Stages of Your Life

Being a workaholic will encompass almost your entire existence as it did mine. I was that happy workaholic for nearly four decades. Each decade brought along its unique challenges and severe heartaches; however, the issues were never enough to bring me to my knees until I lost the love of my life. When that happened, I was scared to death of being alone—especially in my old age. I became chronically depressed, shutting down frequently for hours at a time. Such behavior was unheard of for someone who had always been known as Mr. Productivity.

This recurring pattern went on for almost a year until my co-author and friend Leticia intervened and said something to me that saved my life. In a way that really stirred my heart and soul, she said to me, "You're never alone Harris, God is with you always." There was a bit more to it than that, but that's the gist of it. That simple message *really* hit home. Now my priorities have shifted in a whole different direction: relationships (family and faith), health and career. These were all number one priority now.

My workaholic habits haven't changed much because it's what I love to do. I also still exercise seven days a week like I've always done. The big difference is that worshipping and glorifying God through prayer and kind acts toward others now comes before work. Below is an analysis of how being a workaholic can sabotage the different stages of your life.

Late Teens/Twenties

Starting your workaholic lifestyle at an early age has plenty of benefits, but it can also have some disastrous, ugly negatives. In most instances you're earning a good salary, waking up feeling exhilarated every morning, and growing your knowledge base. But people who work way more than they should are only fulfilled in one area of their lives and are more prone to lose sight of their morals. They become one-dimensional and are incapable of enjoying relationships, family outings and any other kind of social activities.

Sometimes due to your upbringing, you get sucked into being a workaholic and once that happens it's nearly impossible to stop. When I was a teenager, my goal was to find a job prior to finishing high school. My parents instilled in me a strong work ethic and a sense of urgency, which was instrumental in me learning how to make a living early on in my teen years. That stern lecture my father gave me on a regular basis never stopped ringing in my head:

"Son, when you turn 18, and you graduate from high school, you will have to start paying your mother and I rent. If you decide to go to college, you won't have to pay rent, but you will need to find a part-time job to help pay for your meals, clothing, and anything else you're going to need to further your education."

Like so many of my peers, I wasn't sure whether or not to continue my education. After all I wasn't a genius—I had an average IQ. I tried to attend one class at our community college in San Mateo, California, but I didn't complete the course. It took me approximately a month to realize that I wasn't exactly college material. Working and getting paid a good salary was much more appealing and exciting to me.

I went on to have a few part-time jobs but it wasn't enough—I desperately wanted full-time employment. With the help of my mom, who was working as the head cook in the cafeteria of a large corporation in the San Francisco Bay Area, I was able to secure a fulltime entry-level position. She just so happened to be good friends with the Head of the Data Processing Department, a brilliant Jewish man who simply adored her. One morning when he came to the cafeteria for his morning breakfast, my mom struck up a conversation with him. "Hi, Warren. My son who is extremely hard-working is graduating next week from high school and is looking for full-time work—do you have any openings?"

He said to my mother, "Pnina, yes, I do. I will have Donna, my assistant, call your son and setup an interview in the next few days."

One week later I was employed. Yours truly was removing carbon sheets sandwiched in between computer generated paper and making minimum wage doing it.

I will never forget the time I received my first corporate paycheck. I quickly zoomed in on the total amount paid and then looked over at my name—how cool was that? At the moment something inside me just clicked. I wanted more where that came from. It was an undeniable feeling, the ultimate high. Of course I didn't know it at the time, but that turned out to be the pivotal moment when the ultimate workaholic was first conceived. The experience persuaded me to forego my education altogether and try my hand at climbing the corporate ladder without a college degree.

Now I am going to fast forward to the year 1972, when one of the first IBM mainframe computers was rolled into our department's brand-new computer room with an elevated floor and glass all around it. The work space was unreal—a sight to behold. I knew right then and there exactly in which direction I wanted to take my career. For the first few months, I excelled in my position, performing my duties in five hours' time. Due to my efficiency, I quickly got the attention of management, not only because work was completed well so quickly, but because I was helping out in other departments.

Learning everything about Warren's world quickly became my number one priority. I wanted to stay on management's radar screen. All of my hard work paid off: within a year, I was promoted to a senior position. But I was still hungry for more advancement. After a few years more and several promotions, I decided that a career shift was the next bold move I wanted to make. I wanted to get into management, so I set my sights on Warren's job. That's where the big bucks were after all. The following year, I applied for a vacant supervisor's position, which meant I would have to be interviewed by a few managers, including Warren.

Sitting in Warren's office was nerve-racking to say the least. He was always stern. You rarely saw him smile. When he barked out orders, people jumped. During the interview, Warren asked me several questions. One was, "Where do you want to be in your career in the next one to five years?"

I looked him squarely in the eye and said, "My ultimate goal is to be in your shoes."

Warren actually smiled.

The next question he asked was, "What's the single most important qualification for a manager to have?" It was a great question and Warren knew he had me trapped. He went on to say, "There are many qualifications that a manager must have to be a great one, but Harris, I want you to name the single most important one."

Unsure of how to respond, I gave him a lame answer that suggested a great manager has the ability to make his team happy. Warren shook his head and corrected me. "Your number one responsibility is to get the job done and how you do it is up to you."

That was the end of the interview. Warren taught me a valuable lesson that day, one I never forgot. But while I did not totally ace the interview, I got the job anyway. From that day forward, I had something to prove. So there I was, in my twenties, working around the clock to see what I was really made of.

Thirties

You have just hit the thirty-year mark and the whole world seems to be in the palm of your hands. The path to success is within grasp. Your career is soaring to new heights you once believed were impossible to reach. You're waking up with a sense of urgency and a purpose every day. You are raking in the big bucks and your confidence level is at an all-time high. Now brace yourself for some bad news. At this juncture in your life, you're starting to get an ego the size of the Goodyear blimp. The simple things in life no longer satisfy you, so lately you've started to covet the finest things money can buy, like expensive designer clothing, high-dollar cars, and an outrageously priced home. You're climbing the corporate ladder fairly quickly and you have no problem squashing anyone or anything that dares get in your way. Everything outside of work becomes secondary to you, especially relationships.

When you're a workaholic in your thirties, there is little time available for a serious, long-lasting relationship. Even if you think you want to have a meaningful relationship with someone, you are not going to have the time to foster and nurture it. Since your mind and body will crave human companionship from time to time, you will stubbornly keep trying to pursue that perfect relationship, but in the end you are going to realize that your heart, mind and soul aren't really in it because they are consumed with your number one priority. For longer than you care to admit, your entire world has revolved around the one thing that truly excites and challenges you—work. No matter how hard you try, there is no way to turn off this addiction, even if you're with someone special and during the most intimate of times. While you may be able to block it out for thirty minutes or so, it's only a matter of time before you will start feeling withdrawal symptoms. Face it: your mind will always be on work.

At this stage of the game, you may be thinking about getting married and starting a family with someone who you think may be the love of your life. Don't be fooled. Most workaholics who go this route quickly find out that having a spouse and children to take care of is going to get in the way of their career. In a workaholic's life there is only room for one true love and that is normally their work. The powerful addiction they feel simply can't be turned off. Sure, a workaholic may be able to deny his or her true feeling for days, weeks, or even months, in the end they will always cave in to the mega-powerful force that owns them lock, stock, and barrel. For many workaholics, having a continuous love affair with their work is much more time-consuming and rewarding than being in a relationship with another human being.

The biggest hindrance for a workaholic is his or her children. Even having parental responsibilities will not slow a work addict down or put things into the right perspective for him or her. Everyone knows that children are very demanding and rightfully so. They need and deserve their parent's undivided attention. But the number of households with two working parents is at an all-time high. It's no wonder that many children today feel lonely and neglected. As for me, I am the proud father of a son and daughter. When they were young, we went on great family vacations, but unfortunately my mind was always on work. Pathetic, I know. Reflecting on the past, I am truly ashamed to admit that on many occasions I let the opportunity of playing with my son or daughter or watching a movie with them pass me by. Instead of spending quality time with them, I insisted they watch the movie while I sat alongside them, working the whole time.

Forties

Tell me, does this scenario seem familiar to you? Or perhaps you've heard of this happening to someone you know. You are physically living under the same roof with the person you're married too, but your spirit is always floating somewhere else, far, far away. While you may think you're cleverly getting away with it, everyone knows exactly what you are trying to pull off, especially your spouse or significant other. Make no mistake: there will come a time when your spouse will get fed up with the fact that you're always missing in action. Brace yourself because if you don't make an honest effort to change, you're heading straight for a divorce, if you haven't already had one. In all likelihood, after all the smoke has cleared, you will have ended up losing most of your prized possessions such as your nice bank account, fancy car, a secure place to live and about half of your 401K retirement plan. While the material things you've lost can eventually be replaced, the loss of the human beings in your life is something you may never be able to get over.

Dealing with your ex, especially if you have children together, will be a total nightmare. If you think office politics in the corporate world are brutal, you ain't seen nothing yet. One of the most painful things you may have to face is having to share custody of your children with a person whom you've either wronged in a really bad way or now can't stand. Divorce is inevitable for most workaholics who flat-out refuse to change their ways. Chances are if you have amassed a good deal of assets due to your relentless pursuit of that almighty dollar, separating from or divorcing your spouse will be a painful process. One thing you may struggle with is that as a married person, you got used to hoarding a lot of cash. Even though the money was deposited either by you or your spouse into joint accounts, deep down inside you feel as though you played a greater role in generating that income than your spouse did. This kind of mentality will make you feel as though you're more entitled to it than your ex-husband or ex-wife. If getting a divorce is written in the stars for you, the best thing you can hope for is for it to be civil and have a peaceful resolution.

At the end of the day, if you and your ex can be in the same room without throwing daggers at one another, then I'd say you've had a successful divorce, if there is such a thing. But what about those poor unfortunate souls who have no choice but to undergo a complicated divorce in which the custody of several children must be decided and many assets have to be divided fairly? As a workaholic, I had a daily routine which revolved around my work and the constant management of assets. When faced with divorce, my straightforward life was turned upside down. Life as I knew it took a complete 360-degree turn. I lost about everything including my sanity. It truly was a brutal ordeal for me. Don't let this happen to you!

Fifties

If you have managed to live this long and remain in relatively good health—congratulations! You've been blessed. Unfortunately many workaholics aren't that lucky. Being an extremist workaholic has prevented you from taking care of your health—at least that was the excuse *du jour*—every day. I'm willing to bet that you haven't done much in the way of physical activity—if any. More than likely, throughout the years you have missed more doctor appointments than you care to admit and have not eaten healthy on a regular basis. At this stage of your existence, you have come to the grim realization that being a workaholic is extremely harmful to living a longer and healthier life. Now you're trying to change your ways because you know that managing your health now is a matter of do or die.

You would be surprised just how many workaholics are out of shape, but then that doesn't matter to them because they're invincible, powerful and successful and that makes up for not having a good physique. Well, perhaps two out of these three characteristics may be true—none of us are ever really invincible. Let me tell you something, when you are in your fifties and out of shape, then you're a walking time bomb that could explode at any given moment. Don't let this happen to you or anyone else you care about. If you desire to keep on doing what you love and wish to be there for your family for the long haul, then eat right and consistently exercise. In other words, proactively manage your health.

Sixties

That workaholic mentality during your sixties will prevent you from having fun. Instead of living a more balanced lifestyle, which includes a healthy dose of recreational activities, your only recourse is still work. Entertainment, companionship and just plain old relaxation are all nonexistent. Despite all of the warning signs, you still haven't learned to live life. You are a classic example of someone who lives to work when what you should be doing is the exact opposite—work to live.

In some cases being a relentless workaholic becomes a makeshift security blanket, especially for those who have gone through a divorce or two. Trust me when I say that the last thing you want to deal with is more nonsense from another relationship. We all know most relationships start out wonderful, but when both parties involved fall off Cloud Nine, the ending is not so great. This is exactly what happened to me after meeting so many wonderful women. It became so much easier to be alone in peace and quiet than to deal with emotional drama from the opposite sex.

Being totally alone isn't the answer either. It negatively impacted me on several occasions, even while writing this book. I would shut down periodically from severe depression for a few hours at a time, which is very uncharacteristic of me. Occasionally I was an emotional train wreck. It was brutal when it hit. Then I learned that I was never alone. Faith, my work, daily exercise and having fun with my daughter was the right formula for reinventing myself.

In Denial

If you're a workaholic in denial, you may have to enlist the help of a licensed professional counselor who specializes in addiction. The problem is most likely stemming from your childhood experiences. I know that my parents played a major role in my upbringing and workaholic-mentality. Both worked extremely hard. They immigrated to this country from Israel in 1960 and earned everything the old-fashioned way—working long hours and being financially disciplined. They were frugal and saved for a rainy day until eventually they had enough to invest in property.

Working hard and making something happen in our household was a way of life. The difference between my parents and I was that they weren't selfish. They worked hard for the *family's* success, while I went overboard for my own personal gain and selfish pleasures. It was all about Harris Kern. When I became the King of the Mountain, I refused to let the people I most cared about join me at the top. There I was, in total denial, working and exercising hard. To my credit, I didn't smoke, use recreational drugs or drink. I also kept myself in great shape and became successful. So what was so wrong about that? How could I have been headed down a path of self-destruction back then? The answer to these questions is quite simple. Because it was all about me and no one else. I realized it more and more in my late forties, but I kept ignoring the warning signs which were, I always:

- Wanted to be alone
- Ignored family and friends
- Gravitated toward work regardless of the issue
- Looked for a professional ROI not a personal one

If you're in denial the same way I was and you feel you need help to overcome your situation, then it would be advantageous to see a specialist. Being a workaholic is an addiction which will eventually destroy you unless it's treated properly before a major personal disaster happens in your life. (Please refer to the professional help section below.)

What Goes Up Must Come Down

While I was on top of the world, I acted shamelessly and had no morals whatsoever. Not once did I ever stop to look back at all the bad deeds I was responsible for. Who cared anyway? If something wasn't on my daily to-do list and I didn't have time to deal with it, I just swept it under the rug. I was having too much fun in my little workaholic world to bother myself with things that did not directly affect me in any way. What did concern me was collecting more expensive toys, beautiful young girlfriends, and sculpting a better body so I could pick up even more chicks. Then, one unsuspecting day, my empire came crashing down on me very much in the same way an earthquake strikes—it was payback time. God played his hand—life as I knew it ended. The time to bring the high and mighty Harris Kern down to his knees came—the good times were over. I went down hard and nothing or no one could save me, even all my money.

Decades of suppressing my conscience caught up with me and suddenly I felt the need to suffer the same kind of major pain I had inflicted on others. Something inside me shifted, my heart changed so much that it made me arrive at the decision that for the rest of my existence on this planet, I deserved to feel nothing but unbearable pain. However, in time I would learn that just wasn't my call to make. That decision solely belonged to a higher authority and no one else.

The two-priority workaholic path destroyed me. Because of it, I lost my family and my fortune. Thinking about it, I deserved to lose it all. As a result of the reckless way I lived my life, one day I found myself completely alone. The only silver lining was that I still had my name to cling onto. Big whoopee! There I was, a 60-year-old man all alone with his name, not a pretty picture at all. There was no longer a wife to kiss good night or children to drive to school. The only way for me to survive after having lost everything was to bring spirituality back into my life—front and center. When I realized just how disrespectful and loveless I had been to so many, I began to pray hard day and night asking for God's forgiveness. I thought that perhaps He would make the pain and suffering go away quickly. Well, it didn't quite work out that way. God was not about to let me off the hook that easily. I can't say that I blame Him.

Seeking Professional Help

Workaholics will resist seeking professional help, just like I did. My mentality back then was "who has time for that nonsense?" This is how most of us workaholics think. Seeking professional help would be the absolute last resort. It was an action I fought every step of the way. But the minute I stopped resisting and allowed myself to be vulnerable long enough to receive the help I so desperately needed, the quality of my life improved in a short time. Who am I kidding? It actually saved my life. My help came from a friend. Once healthy again, I designed a new strategy to maintain balance in my life.

If you open your mind and heart to the content in this book, it could save your life too—like it did mine. Trust me, I am not using this statement lightly, nor am I overdramatizing a really serious problem. Absorbing and putting into practice what you will learn from reading this book will enable you to be much more productive and happy and allow you to achieve anything you set your mind to.

People who are interested in finding inpatient or outpatient services for workaholism should consider calling 1-800-660-0986, or fill out a quick contact form, which can be downloaded by visiting http://www.addiction-treatment.com/research/work/. This will be a good way for them to receive the help they need. Workaholism is treated like many other addiction problems and in some cases may have to include therapy and medications. A licensed professional counselor or therapist can walk you or another person with this issue through the steps needed to heal and move on with the business of living. Some workaholism stems from other problems, such as alcoholism, and can be addressed by a therapist either in one-on-one or group sessions. During Workaholics Anonymous (WA) meetings, individuals who suspect they have a problem are asked the following questions:

- Is work the activity you like to do the best and do you talk about work all the time?
- Have your family and friends given up hope that you will spend quality time with them or not show up late to important events?
- Do you get irritated when people ask you to stop doing your work so you can help them with something?
- Do you always feel guilty? Guilty for not being with the family? But then feeling guilty for not doing work?

For many workaholics, counseling and therapy in recovery also includes attendance and participation in 12-step meetings. Workaholics Anonymous is a fellowship of individuals who share their experience, hope and strength with each other in order to help solve common problems and work on recovery. The fellowship holds in-person meetings (in the U.S. and a growing list of international locations) as well as online and teleconferences. The website has links which list meeting places that many find helpful. Check out the W.A. literature page for links to books, pamphlets and other helpful information on work addiction and recovery. One of these sources of material is the *Workaholics Anonymous Book of Recovery*, a 230-page soft-bound book available for order through WA's website.

CHAPTER THREE

The Ultimate Workaholic

If you are a manager, then your number one priority should be to get the job done. Naturally, you want the best team money can buy—right? When push comes to shove, who would you hire? A workaholic or a non-workaholic? That's a no-brainer! Of course the only viable answer for you is a workaholic. If given the right incentive, a workaholic will *do whatever it takes* to get the job done, even if that means sacrificing sleep, health, family and everything else that is not associated with getting the job done. I am a classic example of this kind of behavior. I regarded every work project I worked on as being more sacred than the Bible itself. That is unforgiveable, yes, I know. But that just goes to show how my mind operated. What business owner or CEO of a large corporation wouldn't want an employee who thinks with this ideology? In the chapters ahead I will be analyzing what are some of the good, bad, and ugly characteristics workaholics have that define them.

Not Everything is Doom and Gloom

Most workaholics have pretty good self-discipline skills, although their focus is one-dimensional. In other words, they excel in one area and fail miserably in others, putting all of their eggs in one basket. For many of them, eventually, that one basket of theirs turns up empty and they are totally blindsided by it.

As a way of being able to better measure the different levels of the workaholic's most notable positive and negative character traits, I've come up with the following definitions:

- *Good:* Self-driven, productive, goal-oriented, highly ambitious, efficient with resources, urgently hardworking, results-oriented, energetic, focused and with an endless appetite to accomplish tasks.
- *Bad:* Selfish, egotistical, controlling, unhealthy, power-hungry, one-dimensional and with a total disregard for spiritual things.
- *Ugly:* Immoral, unfaithful (to spouse), indifferent and uncaring about friends, and is willing to betray or stab anyone in the back for personal gain in the corporate world.

There seems to be no contest. The bad and ugly characteristics of a workaholic by far trump the good ones. It wouldn't be such a bad picture if workaholics were somehow able to harness the good traits they have and channel their useful skills through to other key areas of their lives, therefore eliminating the bad and ugly characteristics. After having pondered the issue a great deal, in my opinion workaholism is a condition that can be cured, however it will take some effort. It's not going to be easy. I strongly believe there is only one way to successfully treat workaholism and that is by:

- Establishing and adhering to the three most important priorities equally in order to maintain balance: *career*, *health* and *relationships*.
- Incorporating tasks, activities, routines associated with the above priorities on your daily to-do list.
- Practicing sound self-discipline techniques in all three areas.
- Being spiritual.

These four elements will be discussed in detail later on in the prescriptive section of this book.

A Lean, Mean, Working Machine

Most people who know me well say I'm a lean, mean, working machine, because I work around the clock and rarely break down. While it's true I may need occasional maintenance in the form of food and power naps, I just keep on delivering. Like the Energizer Bunny, I just keep beating my own drum. I've trained my mind and body to sleep only four hours a night in order to accomplish more—been doing that for the past four decades without any ill effect. Knock on wood! Throughout the years, I've always felt proud being thought of as a machine by others. For me it symbolizes the ultimate level of productivity and I was well worth every penny my employers invested in me. I was the top of the line as far as machines go. Heck, I was far more dependable than a Maytag washing machine.

On a sad note, being labeled a machine implied that I was an empty, hollow shell of a man incapable of having any feelings or emotions. This was the Frankenstein side of me. What can I say? Everyone was right. After suffering the hardest fall of them all—losing the woman of my dreams because of my machine-like characteristics, I changed my evil ways. I do have feelings, I've always had them. They were just suffocated by my self-serving priorities.

Having a machine-like demeanor can be a very powerful thing. But it can also prove to be deadly. On the positive side, I was and still am relentless, motivated, focused and always productive. Nowadays, the only thing that gets in the way of my deliverables is my family. I'm a constant that never fails. On the negative side, for decades, I didn't have much of a personal life. Now I spend quality time with my family. Granted, I'm afraid to ever have another romantic relationship *ever* again, but this is by choice. Quite frankly, I don't want one. I am content in my life with my faith; my ex-wife, whom I still love; my children; a few close personal friends; my daily exercise regimen and, of course, my work.

While I am proud of my past accomplishments, there is still a great deal more that I wish to accomplish before leaving this world. I still have that same "eye of the tiger" hunger and look that I sported during my corporate glory days. However, I am more balanced now than ever before and I've come too far to revert back to the person I used to be. But that doesn't mean I am going to push all the way forward either. I flat-out refuse to put down the wall that protects my personal world. I will stand behind that strong mural to protect myself from getting emotionally attached to anyone ever again. I am at peace with my decision and that machine-like mentality is here to stay, but *always* with balance.

Workaholism is Great for Your Career

My second corporate mentor who truly made an impact on me is one of the most brilliant men I've had the pleasure of knowing. His name is Mike Graves. He ran the IT department at Sun Microsystems, a multi-billion dollar manufacturer of networked technology solutions. Mike had more than 1,000 employees working for him, located all over the world. He was the top dog in IT—pretty much unapproachable until you earned his respect.

Most of Mike's employees and other members of his organization were afraid of him—even yours truly, before I got to know him better. He would constantly bark out unrealistic demands. At the time, there were hundreds of business-critical projects that needed to be implemented ASAP due to the explosive growth of the business. Unfortunately in IT, there were always more projects than available resources. Mike had a very loud and stern voice. He was also very direct. His projects were typically massive and their deadlines were always a priority. Mike was all about high performance and quality. If you wanted recognition you needed to constantly produce. I eventually grew to admire the man and learned a great deal from him.

In order to be on Mike's management team, you had to consistently excel in a major way. It wasn't enough to be just another workaholic. He had plenty on his staff. As a matter of fact, all of his direct reports had to be workaholics to keep up with his unrealistic demands. They always accomplished their tasks on schedule. I wanted to stand out by outperforming everyone else on his senior management team. I was the youngest by at least ten years.

In those days, I had a lot of *chutzpah* and everyone knew it. My *chutzpah* was used in the politically correct manner. I learned how to play the corporate politics game well so I wouldn't alienate anyone. I was confident, but at the same time very respectful of others. It's that discipline of mine that took me to different levels. I was more energetic and driven than anyone else. Mike was about to witness that firsthand. The rest of his management team was also going to know who Harris Kern truly was. What I wanted most of all back then was a VP slot so I could report directly to Mike. There I was, two levels down the management chain, and I wasn't about to wait several years for that promotion. Although I was just a mid-level manager, I was already stirring the pot. The rumors about me began to spread like wildfire and eventually Mike got wind of all the great things I was making happen.

Never Stop Strategizing

I've always been a firm believer that one should continuously strategize to be successful. Whether it's looking for faster ways to complete a project or for career advancement, especially during what I refer to as dead zone times (commuting to work, being in a meeting that's politically motivated and has no real substance or value, waiting for your doctor's appointment). I was always lashing out at myself mentally to figure out how to beat that next deliverable's due date. It didn't matter if it was day or night, I constantly strategized on how to be more efficient. By the way, I place this characteristic under the *good* category because it's truly an asset if you can utilize the same focus in other areas of your life.

Since I worked at a large corporation with thousands of other employees, the pressure was always on to come up with strategic ways of how to climb the corporate ladder ahead of the pack. Over and over again the following litany of questions kept hammering in my brain:

- What is the next move I should make?
- Which position can I get promoted into that will give me more power and a bigger paycheck?
- Who is my greatest competition and how do I get rid of him or her?
- What new skills do I need to master to get ahead?
- What is my plan of attack?

One thing you must always remember is that there is a great deal of competition for that much coveted management slot. In the take-no-prisoner atmosphere that is prevalent in today's corporate world, it's always a major battle for the elite positions. They are limited and far and few between. The question is: How badly do you want that promotion? As for me, I desperately wanted every promotion I set my sights on. The gears in my head were always turning and strategizing at a high RPM. Come rain, sleet or snow, I was always planning the next career move, reviewing organization performance or trying to think of ways to implement a key project faster and under budget. Even when my body was somewhere besides the office, perhaps at a family function, my mind was *always* back at the office.

Back then, if you happened to be having a conversation with me, while I may have appeared to be listening, the truth is it was going in one ear and out the other. Honestly, I could care less about what you were saying because to me it was all irrelevant. I became quite the pro at pretending to care and being physically present at family and social events when I absolutely had to. After decades of ongoing practice, my mind became quite efficient of taking a leave of absence at will so I can strategize on what mattered the most to me instead. There was no way you would have been able to catch me in the act (unless you really knew me, like my family did) because I was so damn good at hiding my actual agenda. The key to success in every facet of life is to always strategize about accomplishing your goals faster.

Now let's get back to my story about Mike. Reporting to Mike became an obsession for me. If I only relied on high performance, hard work and quality deliverables it would still have taken me six-plus years to reach my goal of being able to report to him. I wanted that to happen in two years. The company was growing at an incredible pace. It was in the forefront of the Internet boom in the 1990s. I knew there would be constant opportunities and reorganizations: Mike's staff would grow. Therefore I wanted to be on his mind and on the tip of his tongue when it was time to grow his direct reports.

The way I figured it, there was only one way to meet my major goal of moving up the management chain that quickly. In any large organization that is growing there are always initiatives that could be undertaken to improve efficiency and morale. My wheels were turning nonstop to find that one massive initiative that would catapult my career. Mike's direct reports were well-respected by him. For me to get on his radar I would have to be recognized by them as a team player who always did superior work even when I was at my worst. It all had to begin with Paul, my boss.

Winning over My Boss

At this point in my career, I reported to the Director of IT Operations. His name was Paul Roman. He was highly educated, hard-working, and always delivered, come what may. He totally loved his job. Paul was also personable and his laugh was highly infectious. Everyone loved the guy. You really couldn't ask for a better boss. One of the things I most remember about Paul was that he was a baseball fanatic. He would play with his buddies and son every weekend during all four seasons of the year. That's all he ever spoke about. As a matter of fact, if he could have found a way to do it, Paul would've played the game during his lunch break too. But unfortunately his heavy workload wouldn't allow it, until one day I decided to change his life and mine. I went into his office one evening to shoot the breeze with him as he was wrapping things up after a long day.

Paul worked in the office right next to mine. He came to rely on me for just about everything. I was his right-hand man. On this particular evening, life changed for Paul when I said to him, "I want you to play ball every day. I've been working for you for several months now and in that time have you ever had to tell me what to do?"

Paul looked at me with an odd look on his face and replied, "No."

I went on to tell him, "You never will have to tell me what to do. I can handle anything that comes up."

Paul smiled at me with a twinkle in his eyes and said, "It's all yours, Harris."

From that day forward you could see Paul playing catch with his buddies at lunch time. He loved having me around because I made his world easier and more enjoyable. With me holding down the fort, he only had to work forty hours a week, primarily because I lived at work. I had won Paul over. Eventually Mike took notice of the fact that Paul was playing baseball during lunchtime on a daily basis. Not long after that, Mike got wind that while I was running his world, Paul was having the time of his life.

Winning over His Boss

Sam Rangole was Paul's boss. He was the Vice President of IT Operations. He was also an intelligent and hard-working man, who I held in the highest regard. His organization consisted of approximately 400 employees. Sam was in his early fifties. Paul and Sam had a great relationship. Because of it, Sam was now learning more about me and what I was capable of accomplishing. I was starting to make a name for myself by delivering projects *ahead of schedule* and taking on initiatives that weren't assigned to me initially.

Sam's office was two down from mine. Obviously he had the larger corner office. All VPs had the larger corner offices—I wanted one too. Unbeknownst to many of my colleagues, I was ready to start my secret initiative—a humungous project that no one knew about. If I executed it just right, this project was sure to get Paul's, Sam's and eventually Mike's attention. It was a huge training initiative that had not been budgeted for or even identified as a viable project. It was an undertaking that would have an immediate ROI by improving moral and save the organization a significant amount of time and money.

Our company had a large computer room (data center) equipped with a ton of technology to run our entire network and software applications (such as manufacturing and payroll). The room was almost the size of a football field. There were three shifts and a staff of fifteen people supporting all the technology twenty-four hours a day. At the time most of the technology that ran our corporate applications was being stored on Hewlett Packard hardware, in which the staff was well-versed.

One day the top brass made a strategic business decision to replace the existing technology with IBM. Along with that technology decision came a people-component dilemma. The existing data center staff would have to be replaced or re-trained to support these new systems. Training existing personnel to support this type of technology instead of the old HP equipment would have been a tremendous expense to the company and still wouldn't have provided the organization with an experienced enough senior staff to support the new equipment. We would need one senior person per shift to deal with any complex problems that could arise. For the data center staff, the writing was on the wall, their tenure clearly in jeopardy. Moral amongst the staff reached an all-time low, fast. They were going to be laid off once the new systems were up and running. There was no way the company was going to train the existing staff. It wouldn't have been a financially wise decision.

Story: The Mother of All Projects

In a nutshell, my goal was to train the entire Operations Staff—all fifteen people—so no one would be laid off. It was an unrealistic and crazy goal, but I didn't want to wait six-plus years to report to Mike. These individuals knew the business, our clients, and they worked hard. I didn't tell anyone—I just did it. Despite me already working an exorbitant number of hours, I took on the mother of all projects. But I felt that in order to have Mike and all of his direct reports know who Harris Kern was and in a hurry, this was the most effective approach to make it happen.

The strategy I had in mind was two-phased. The first step was for the staff to get acquainted with the new hardware. When it was first rolled into the Data Center it made the entire staff nervous and they were scared to get near it. They reacted like they had been thrust into a war and the enemy had just brought out its newest and greatest technology. It was all so foreign to them. The second phase was for the staff to get familiar with the operating system. The four key goals for this massive project were:

- **Facilitate an evaluation for each of the data center employees** to determine their strengths and weaknesses, self-discipline skills, leadership capabilities, goals and career objectives and technical skills. I wanted to get an idea of how quickly they could learn new technology. I didn't want to waste my time or theirs if they didn't have the desire to take on something new.
- **Develop a beginner's (hands-on) training curriculum with homework assignments to be executed on the new technology.** The key success factors for this type of initiative was to make the team feel comfortable with the new equipment in their own habitat.
- **Develop intermediate and advanced (hands-on) training curricula with homework assigned to be executed on the new technology.**
- **Develop a one-day hardware workshop.** I called

it *"Get Acquainted with the Hardware."* I had the IBM Systems Engineer (SE) assigned to our company come in and teach the staff key components of the hardware in a classroom setting for four hours. For the next four hours, everyone (IBM, SE and the Operations Staff) came into the data center, took apart the new equipment and slapped it back together again. Management couldn't believe that I had done it.

Back in those days, I had a fairly large 12' by 14' office. Let me tell you I used every square inch of floor space. I had a stack of paper (evaluations, homework assignments, curriculum) for each staff member in the computer room. I also purchased a cot and brought a sleeping bag from home to sleep in my office for the next few months. I only went home two to three times a week and only long enough to get fresh, clean clothes and check in with my family. The project consumed me day and night. Sam and Paul were totally blown away by this massive project which, incidentally, was started strictly on my own time.

Paul and Sam would have to walk by my office to get to theirs and of course they saw the cot, sleeping bag, suitcase of clothes, and stacks of paper all over the floor. They couldn't believe what I was doing. I was working around the clock with the team along with doing my job. Word quickly got to Mike and even HR, which was located down the same hall from us.

Once I finished developing the training programs, I worked with the staff on their shifts to provide hands-on training. I was working on this training program and at the same time performing my job responsibilities as a manager. I only believed in hands-on training programs. That's how I learned the IBM technology years previously. It's the most effective method, but also the most time-consuming.

I even went as far as to design custom homework assignments daily for each person. They would receive their homework and provide me with a printout of their results. If they did well, the next homework assignment was going to be more challenging for them. If they didn't do well, I would sit and work with them to understand where they went wrong until they grasped the assignment. No one could believe I was doing this—especially upper management. My plan was working beautifully and smoothly. It felt good because I was training a group of intelligent people to learn a new technology, which would save their livelihood. It also felt good to be recognized by the top dog himself. My students saw what I had sacrificed, which was pretty much my entire life for approximately three months. They had written memos to HR and Mike—incredible memos heralding what I was doing for them.

Story: The Meeting that Changed My Life

It was a typical work night around 7 P.M. when the phone rang—it was an internal call. The ring tone was different for internal calls. Caller ID read: M. Graves. This was a first, Mike calling me. Typically Mike would call Sam or Paul if he wanted something from me or my team. I was shocked and a bit nervous to say the least. This was a highly unusual move for Mike to make. I picked up the receiver and he called me into his office. He knew perfectly well I was still working. Everyone knew that. When I arrived at his office he was sitting there with his legs crossed over his desk. He told me to come in, sit down, and to close the door.

I sat down at his big round coffee table and put my feet up as well. He looked at me and smiled, his way of acknowledging that I had a lot of *chutzpah*. "So, Mr. Kern, I've been hearing about the unbelievable work you've been doing—what do you want out of your career?"

I looked at him and with a confident voice I said to him, "I want your job."

Mike immediately countered, "I like that. You don't beat around the bush, do you?"

"No, sir, I don't. Time is scarce and precious."

From that point forward we hit it off big-time. I could just tell that he really liked me. Mike then said to me, "What I'm about to tell you is strictly confidential."

I replied, "Okay, what you say will stay in this room."

Mike then proceeded to let the cat out of the bag. "I'm going to reorganize and start a new team that reports directly to me. It will be approximately 300 employees with facilities located all over the world that you would be responsible for. Can you handle that?"

Again, I looked him squarely in the eyes and said, "You know I can. When do we start?"

"I'll let you know in a few weeks," Mike said.

At last, this was the vice president position I was waiting for. Two weeks later, I was promoted to that coveted VP slot, reporting directly to Mike, managing more than 300 employees with mini-data centers all over the world. My corporate career had finally been solidified. Was I through working like a maniac? Not by a long shot! I still wanted to squeeze more juice out of my career.

Exemplifying a Corporate Image

Day after day, I was the first to arrive at work and the last to leave. I had an ego, but kept it to myself and always in check. I wanted to be more efficient and powerful than my peers. However, working on things that were assigned by management made me no different than everyone else. I was constantly looking for ways to produce results better, faster and under budget. Basically, I had three goals:

1. My number one goal was to get the job done—doing whatever it took to accomplish that and being recognized as the "go-to guy."
2. My number two goal was to beat the advertised scheduled due date of any project. I had trained my mind that just meeting a project's scheduled due date was not good enough.
3. My third goal was to proactively look at ways to make improvements in overall organization performance without being told to do so. I used to tell my management, "If you have to tell me what to do, then I don't deserve my job or yours."

If I accomplished those three goals consistently I would *always* be on management's radar screen, especially when there was an opportunity for a promotion.

You Can't Stress Me Out—I Put Pressure on Myself

Regardless of the deadline, complexity or grandness of any project, you simply can't put any pressure on a true-blue workaholic to deliver. Most workaholics don't need any kind of outside interference because they put pressure on themselves to outperform their previous best every single day. I am a classic example of this kind of mentality. Come hell or high water, I couldn't be rattled by unrealistic due dates. If my boss assigned a date on a project that was clearly farfetched, I still found a way to get it done ahead of schedule. Once the job was done, to gloat I would make a sarcastic remark such as, "Can't you do better than that?" or "Bring it all on!"

Mike loved the show I put on for his benefit—it was nonstop entertainment for him. As for me, I just wanted to keep accomplishing great feats. My *never enough* mentality refused to let up for even a second. This line of reasoning is what made me so valuable as an employee. But in time this mentality became poisonous and it eventually brought me down. My overwhelming need and addiction to outperform completely took over my life. It spiraled out of control and didn't stop until I lost everything and everyone I cared about.

Project Heaven

During the pinnacle of my career as a corporate executive, the more highly visible projects that were thrown my way, the more turned on I got. I wanted the exposure badly. That is why I multitasked on several projects at the same time. I absolutely loved the workload and unrealistic deadlines. I embraced critical projects that came with the most aggressive deadlines much like a mother cradles her newborn baby—yes, it was that great of an adrenalin rush for me. Anything that wasn't work-related went straight to the bottom of the totem pole. As a result of my superior job performance, I was given two promotions in three years, which was a great achievement.

I never much cared for vacations to exotic destinations, because, in my opinion, they were always short-lived. For me nothing was as exhilarating as turning in a major project ahead of schedule. Don't get me started on how I reacted when someone tried to get me away from my computer, even if it was for just a short while. Being the ultimate workaholic that I was, well, you can imagine how much it hurt me. It felt like my brains, heart and soul were being ripped out of my body. My entire existence and outlet all rested on my work. It was all so pathetic, I know. What can I say? I was head over heels in love with my life as a workaholic. But little did I know that this mentality was going to rear its ugly head one day and stop me in my tracks.

Determined to be Successful at All Costs

It's a well-known fact that approximately 90 percent of all the world's assets belong to 1 percent of the earth's population. Many individuals will do just about anything to excel in their career to be associated with this elite group. This includes, but is not limited to, hard work, maneuvering the politics well and schmoozing with the right executives. I hated playing all the political games that came along with the job, but in order to thrive in the corporate world one has to excel in this highly difficult sport. Yes, I refer to it as a sport because the competition is fierce and there's always a clear-cut winner and loser. It's always a high stakes game of do or die! Working effectively (including thriving in politics) and being ultra-productive will typically get you a nice bonus and perhaps a promotion as well. Achieving this objective at all costs always came first and foremost with me. Everything, including my family, was placed on the back burner. It didn't bother my conscience a bit to do this because I believed with all my heart that the more I accomplished, the bigger the pot of gold would be waiting for me at the end of the rainbow.

Politically Astute

To survive and thrive in the corporate world one has to be shrewd, observant, and have the gift of gab. As I said, I truly detested having to deal with all the political red tape because nothing ever seemed to get done—just like in Washington DC. Whether you work in the private or public sector, the larger the company, the greater the political battlefield. Most of the time having to follow company protocol is such a complete waste of time but you can't just ignore the rules either. Doing so will get you defeated in no time at all. You either have to play the game and do it well or simply move aside so you won't get trampled by those who are in the game to win it. It's that simple!

Even though I didn't like playing the game, I was pretty damn good at it. My objective was to come out as the victor of every heated battle. I never wanted to be blindsided. Listen to someone who knows: it takes a lot of resources to maneuver through all the corporate bullshit. That's why I hated it so much. I could have accomplished a great deal more, but unfortunately playing the political game consumes probably half of a manager's time. I'll say it again: it's the only way to survive and thrive.

Story: The Well-Connected, Unpleasant Manager

It was a typical hectic day at work in the world of IT: resolving problems, dealing with irate computer users and absorbed by people issues. Every organization usually has one person you just love to hate, a genuine pain in the rear end. We had several at this particular company, but one of them stood out from the crowd. She imposed a huge barrier every time we had a new project to implement. This particular person was unanimously hated among all the managers and most of the employees, but no one could do anything about it because she had been with the company for more than fifteen years, knew the right people in HR, skated around the issues and played politics extremely well.

For the sake of anonymity, let's call this person Sandy. Many of us had no choice but to interact with her frequently. Sandy was that roadblock everyone had to get past in order to get anything accomplished. Everyone knew it; it was not just a personality conflict between Sandy and me. Something had to be done about her, so I did what any other red-blooded American would do: I complained to my boss.

Since Mike was always in meetings, the best way to contact him was by email. That particular morning, I sent him an email. By that evening there was no response from him in my inbox, which was highly uncharacteristic of Mike. In most cases, he would respond to his email by the end of the day, but today, something just did not feel right. My curiosity got the best of me so I decided to visit Mike in his office. Although he was my boss, we had a mutual bond and respect for one another. He respected me for my drive, tenacity, sense of urgency and overall discipline, and I for his intelligence and being a visionary. Mike was one of the most brilliant men I've ever known.

It was around 7:00 P.M. His days were usually quite long, just like mine. He was used to hearing about problems and complaints frequently and I was sure this day's set of problems was no different to him from any other. Therefore, I went to his office to discuss one more issue with him, a rather complicated one. As I entered his office, we had a cordial exchange of greetings, and then I sat at his visitor's table, propped my feet up on his table, as I had done many times before and said, "Hey, bud, what's going on?"

"It's been a rough day, Harris. I just read your email. So what are you trying to tell me, that Sandy is a bitch and a major pain in the ass?"

"Yup! Mike, we can't move forward with many of our projects because of this one individual. Most of my organization is frustrated," I explained.

Mike leaned back in his chair. He had known all along that Sandy was a big problem, but he never had the time to deal with it before. Actually, he didn't care to deal with it. Like I said, she knew the right people—especially a senior manager in HR. You could tell by the look on his face that Mike was not lying when he said it had been a bad day for him. He looked at me with a tired look on his face and said, "Harris, you resolve this."

I said, "What? You have to be joking. Sandy is the most hated person within the organization and doesn't even report to me." If she had reported to me in the first place, then, sure, I would have resolved it myself and never had gone to Mike.

I complained bitterly for several minutes. Mike looked straight into my eyes and asked, "Can you deal with it?" I stared right back at him and thought about why he was putting it back on my shoulders. I knew he was doing it for a reason. He was always testing me and mentoring me to improve my management skills, providing me (that's a nice way of putting it) with the most challenging problems—or, shall I say, opportunities.

In retrospect everything Mike threw at me was a good learning experience. I was his student and studied his every move: the way he wrote email, the way he spoke and conducted himself in meetings. It was an innate desire on my part to learn from the best. As I mentioned earlier, Mike Graves has been one of the greatest mentors in my life. Back then I wanted to learn everything I could from this man but I never had the courage to come and say it out loud to him. He was definitely my role model.

Besides admiring me as an employee, Mike liked me as a friend, but he never would admit it. Right then and there, I decided to call his bluff and stared right back at him. "Not only will I handle it, but I'll turn Sandy completely around to be productive instead of always being confrontational with everyone. End of discussion." Before leaving his office, I turned back and said to him, "Oh, one more thing, Have a nice night." In return, Mike looked at me and smirked in the same sly way he always did.

Sandy had an abrasive and obnoxious personality. It was rather easy to get into a fight with her. There were plenty of times when I wanted to. Oh, what a challenge it was to maintain my self-control. What was I getting myself into? The next day I contacted Sandy for a meeting. Judging by her voice, she seemed surprised and leery, to hear from me out of the blue. I kept saying to myself repeatedly, "Why did I accept this crazy challenge?" My workload was already too much for one individual to handle. Why do I always have to challenge myself in this manner needlessly?

The answer was really quite simple. The only viable explanation was that the ultimate workaholic in me and unrelenting self-discipline of mine asking for yet another challenge. I was that jungle cat on the prowl for its next fresh kill. If I could turn this negative situation with Sandy around, it would be quite rewarding and beneficial for everyone. Heck, I would be looked at as the company hero for years to come. On that day, another goal was born.

No one but Mike knew about "Operation Sandy." If I failed, there would have been nobody to blame but myself. The responsibility to turn this person around was solely in my hands. I owned this problem. Mike was telling me, although not in these exact words, *Harris, this is your problem. You have more to gain than anyone else, so don't hand it over, and expect me to resolve it for you.*

I had no idea what I was going to say to Sandy. I kept rehearsing my opening line repeatedly, but nothing made sense to me. When we finally did meet, I got the epiphany of just telling her the truth. Up until then, I have always been cordial to her, saying the obligatory "Good morning" when running into her, or striking up a small conversation in the hallway. She had always been friendly towards me. That's what made it even more difficult for me. When work was not the main topic of conversation, she was actually fine to deal with.

After exchanging a cordial handshake and saying hello, I started the conversation going by giving her the standard line, "I bet you're wondering why I called this meeting."

"Yes," Sandy replied.

"I called this meeting because of the friction between our organizations," I said to her. "Whether you know it or not, there is a wall; maybe not an intentional wall, but a wall nonetheless. We really need to start working together as a team. I'm sure you have issues that affect my group and me. Why don't we see if we can resolve them together?"

Sandy's next comment totally surprised me. "I would like that," she said.

She somehow turned the tables on me. Now it was my turn to be leery of her because she knew how to play the corporate politics game well, so for all I knew this could have been the standard line she gave everyone who tried to challenge her. In that instant, I decided to go out on a limb and tell Sandy that her personality was causing conflict.

"I truly don't want to come off as being disrespectful, but there's more," I said. "Your personality in dealing with business issues, for whatever reason, comes off as confrontational. It puts up huge barriers and causes friction between different groups, making people very uncomfortable and on the defensive. Now maybe I am reading it wrong, so please help me out here. We are two grown adults in management positions, so there is no reason why we cannot work on this issue together."

Finally, I had spoken my mind. I had put it all out there. I had no idea what Sandy was going to say next, but at least the truth came out.

There I stood, waiting for her to pop me one, tell me to get out of her office, or worse, threaten that she was going to report me to her friend in HR. Instead of backing down, I continued to speak about how everyone felt about her. She did not seem all that surprised.

When I was finished talking something really strange happened, which really threw me for a loop. Sandy humbled herself and asked if I could help her change.

I responded, "I'd love to."

For the next few months, my weekly mentoring sessions with Sandy took place. Everyone was surprised, but no one more than me. I saw her change from being a hindrance to becoming a valuable asset to the company. It was truly rewarding to see that transformation take place before my very eyes. Sure, I had completed my goal—I never doubted for a minute that I wouldn't. In the grand scheme of things that was irrelevant, what truly mattered was that I had helped a fellow human being improve herself. This felt a whole lot better than just accomplishing a short-term goal. To me, this accomplishment was the equivalent of having completing two goals. Through it all I learned the importance of taking responsibilities upon myself instead of dumping them on someone else and I have Mike to thank for this.

Story: Exercising and Schmoozing with the Big Boss

The more time I spent with Mike, the more I learned from him. He was an excellent leader. As a bonus, our personalities were very similar so we bonded nicely. But I also had a hidden agenda. The more I bonded with him, the likelier I was to get a promotion and larger bonus. Finally, the time had come for me to put my plan into motion. All of my peers in Mike's organization knew I worked out at the Decathlon Club in Santa Clara, California every morning at 5 A.M., when the club opened. Actually I was always there by 4:45 A.M.to make sure I was the first one in the door, otherwise I'd have to waste time waiting in line to check in. They had a slow and antiquated system to check people in. Corporate had an account with the Decathlon Club and as a result a good number of employees would go exercise there on a daily basis. It was conveniently located in the heart of Silicon Valley—the technology capital of the world.

Back then my workouts were always high octane, just like they are today. Every time I was done with my workout it felt awesome. At first I felt drained, but after showering, I was always ready to kick some major butt. My daily workouts made me feel like I was on top of the world—every morning. Confidence spewed from my veins, which made me a force to be reckoned with at work. Now if working out for 1.5 hours every morning wasn't enough, I also used to run at lunch time several times a week during the spring, summer and fall months. It felt so great and liberating. I also used to go hiking with several of the managers once a week—that included Mike, who was a fierce competitor. He also knew that I was the ultimate competitor in exercise. Just like with work, I always wanted to outdo my previous best.

One evening I was shooting the breeze with Mike in his office. We were having a conversation about exercise. I wasn't afraid to say anything to Mike with the door closed. I respected him and he respected me. One day out of the blue I said, "Hey, Mike, you're almost fifty years old, when are you going to get rid of that gut? It looks like shit!"

Mike smirked at me and said, "I'm starting to exercise a few days a week."

"A few days a week is nothing. You need to go daily," I said to him. "Why don't you come work out with me and I'll show you how to use the equipment."

"Okay, you're on," Mike replied.

The next morning Mike was at the gym promptly at 4:45 A.M. When the club opened, we went straight for the weights. He wasn't about to let me see that he was wimpy... This was a man thing and he wanted to prove a point. Only Mike forgot one thing—you just can't go right for the heavy weights without feeling some MAJOR pain the next day. But Mike didn't care—he kept up with me. We actually had fun working out together. It was very intense—when we finished I knew he would be hurting in the morning and he was.

After a few weeks of working out together, my plan worked. I soon became Mike's favorite employee. I was helping him get into shape and he was teaching me a great deal about leadership and corporate politics. It was a win-win situation, especially for me, because I eventually became a senior vice president. To think, much of how I climbed to that plateau came from earning my dues with hard work, eventually becoming the department's go-to person and bonding with Mike.

Summarizing the Good Characteristics

Workaholics have a willingness to consistently work long hours to meet unrealistic deadlines. They will also place a company's interest before their personal obligations and feelings. That's what distinguishes a successful workaholic from the rest of the workers. Execution in these areas is the key to securing a position in upper management or a large bonus every year. The problem is that these good characteristics sometimes impede sound judgment. You become so focused on taking these characteristics to the next level that you forget about everything else that's so important in life. Faith, balance, and discipline are the key ingredients for ensuring you don't become that ultimate workaholic like me who destroyed his family and life.

CHAPTER FOUR

The Bad and the Ugly

After reading this section, ask yourself: How can anyone survive being a workaholic? Surprisingly many people do for years until they fall hard. A hopeless workaholic will turn a blind eye to the warning signs. Even though he or she may have heard or know of them, they ignore all the red flags—just like I did. It's not like I was completely oblivious to my bad and ugly side. I was merely too busy and I thought myself to be immune from any negative fallout from my behavior. In a way, I guess you could say I was living in a fantasy land of my own making. Below, I've listed some of the bad traits I possessed and the habits of other workaholics I've been associated with either as a life coach, working in start-up businesses, or an executive in the corporate world.

Living an Unhealthy Lifestyle

Workaholics rarely take the time to exercise. The number one excuse they use for not taking care of their health is, "I'm busy." This is why most workaholics are out of shape. Other excuses they give is, "I travel too much for work or I'm always too tired to exercise." Back in the day, when I traveled extensively, it never ceased to amaze me how many heavyset executives I saw with their roller bags in tow, cruising on the convenient automated walkways instead of actually walking briskly on their own two feet through airports. Come on now... who doesn't get tired after a long day of traveling? By doing the following two things, I was able to not let my fatigue get in the way of exercising. I always made it a point to exercise before getting on an airplane even if I had an early morning flight. Granted, I would get minimal sleep that night, but when I got on the plane, I was exhausted and fell asleep easily. Oftentimes when I traveled internationally, I wouldn't be able to sleep so instead of tossing and turning in bed, I got up and headed straight for the gym. If it wasn't open, I would ask the hotel management to let me have access to it.

Humans weren't made to sit at a desk for eight or more hours a day without getting some form of cardiovascular activity. The sad thing is many workaholics do it for more than 12 hours at a time without any real movement. Ideally, we should all be exercising at least thirty minutes a day to help keep the doctor away. In addition to reducing the risk for nearly every major disease, exercise has been shown to help fight anxiety and depression. It's no wonder that workaholics are more likely to have health issues, such as high blood pressure, irritability, fatigue, and headaches. Personally, I like exercising in the morning because it gets my brain stimulated quickly. It wakes me up in a big way. I am much more alert as soon as I get to the office. I don't need three cups of coffee to wake up after I've exercised.

Poor Eating Habits

Most of the time, die-hard workaholics work well into the evening. When the pangs of hunger start to nag at them, they typically go for some kind of unhealthy fast food like pizza, burgers, or even poorly prepared Chinese cuisine to quiet down their growling stomachs. The next thing you know they become 10, 20 or 30 pounds overweight and can no longer see their own toes much less bend down to touch them. Sure they may be doing brilliant work, but what good is all that when they are digging themselves an early grave and making their families worry to death about them in the process. If you happen to fit this description, you may want to start thinking about how you can change your habits so that you are around long enough to enjoy the fruits of your labor.

Many workaholics drink too much and end up being alcoholics. It is okay to drink moderately (1 to 2 drinks daily) for socializing, but more than that is purely unhealthy. Just because you may consider yourself to be a successful workaholic, don't think for a moment that by drinking more than you should, you're not causing irreparable internal damage to your body. Women who are not pregnant should limit themselves to one drink a day.

Poor Health Management

Missing my annual physical checkup was standard operating procedure for this workaholic. My most-used line for postponing my yearly visit to the doctor was, "I'll eventually get to it—I'm swamped with work right now." Realistically speaking, when wasn't I swamped with work? When I turned fifty years old, common sense, not to mention my loving wife, dictated I was supposed to go in for a colonoscopy. But I kept putting it off every year until I hit the age of 55. By this time my wife was so fed up with my nonchalant attitude that she finally forced the issue and made me go. Despite all the kicking and screaming I did, she practically dragged me to the doctor's grasping my hand the whole time. Don't let this happen to you!

Always Working Through Illness

Before the Internet came along, missing a day of work due to illness was simply unheard of for a workaholic. This unstoppable workaholic never missed a day of work, even when I had a severe cold, which, like most people, I did an average of twice a year. Instead of staying home and resting, I would go into the office, even if I was highly contagious. It was wrong to spread my germs around and contaminate others in the office, but that's how selfish I had become. I only thought about myself and my high-profile projects with those aggressive deadlines. I didn't care about anything else or other human beings. I knew perfectly well that when one is sick their productivity level drops off considerably and the best medicine is getting extra rest. But it didn't matter a hill of beans to me. I just couldn't stay away from the office. It's different now in this era since there's instantaneous access to the Internet nearly everywhere you go. A workaholic can work from home no matter how sick they may be. It's just a matter of bringing their laptop to bed with them.

Sleeping Less

Since I was always thinking about work, sleeping never came easily for me. Taking a sleeping pill or two only knocked me out for a few hours at a time, but unfortunately, that would be all the sleep I got. Pills always did have very little impact on me. The same can be said about a natural sleeping aid like Melatonin—it only helped for a few hours. My mind was a labyrinth of thoughts—always racing and thinking about what was on my plate for the next day. While everyone in my household was sleeping peacefully at night, I strategized incessantly in the dark on how to climb the corporate ladder faster. The wheels just kept on spinning even though my body was exhausted. It was a switch I just couldn't turn off.

My inner voice kept telling me that I was playing Russian roulette with my body by reducing the number of hours I slept. To me it was merely a game of mind over matter. To buy myself more time, I was always trying to sleep the bare minimum. For some crazy reason I became fixated on the number four. I didn't want to sleep more than four hours a night. This was so asinine. I realize that now. But that's how obsessed I was about accomplishing more.

Everyone needs ample good quality sleep. We all know that. Six to seven hours should be the bare minimum—even for tough workaholics. Any less sleep on a consistent basis could cause memory issues, irritability, fatigue and difficulty concentrating. I was a fool taking it to the ultimate extreme by cutting my sleep to four hours a night for more than three decades. People used to ask me all the time: "Why would you sleep so little?" My usual response was, "I have way too much to accomplish in life. Besides, I will sleep plenty when I die."

Sleep was an evil necessity for me so I trained my mind to hold myself accountable to do with less. Clearly, it wasn't one of my best ideas, but I felt invincible—stupid, I know. But this just goes to show the extent of my workaholic mentality. Luckily, God was watching over me and everything appears to be functioning properly. Despite all the self-imposed constant physical abuse I endured all those years, I don't think I caused too much damage. Knock on wood!

Incapable of Relaxing

Relax is a four-letter word to any self-respecting workaholic. It's a well-known fact that the harder you work without getting sufficient rest, the more likely you will eventually succumb to stress. We all know that out-of-control stress can cause high blood pressure, weight loss or gain, recurring headaches, sleeping disorders and chest pains among other symptoms. Make no mistake, for a normal hardworking individual, stress can be a deadly adversary and it shouldn't be taken lightly.

For workaholics stress is just a natural part of the world they love so much. In fact, if their workload was to suddenly fall off the face of the earth never to be seen or heard from again, some workaholics would prefer to die of a heart attack or stroke due to incredibly high stress levels that would stem from having no work. They wouldn't know what to do with themselves. This is sad but so very true. I was no different. It was extremely difficult for me to turn the working machine inside of me completely off.

Sometimes the only way I could relax for a short while was to watch something on television with my wife and children. There were two television shows that I watched occasionally which were so silly I could only stomach thirty minutes of uninterrupted viewing at a time. These two shows really did the trick for me though. One was *WWE Wrestling*. Even though I knew all the wrestling matches had been orchestrated, it was still highly entertaining to watch. Every bout that was featured pitted a good guy versus a bad one. There was no real mystery about it, just good ol' fashioned entertainment, nothing more. The other show I liked to watch was the widely popular sitcom *Married with Children*. These two TV shows were the only form of entertainment that could stop the wheels in my mind from turning for a short time.

Story: Paradise in the South Pacific

Even while on vacation, I was always thinking about work. My body may have physically been on that beautiful white sandy beach in the middle of paradise, but my mind was back at the office. I couldn't wait to get back to civilization to check my voicemails, look at my email every morning and dozens of times throughout the day. I specifically recall an incredible excursion I experienced in the Philippines after doing a presentation for hundreds of CEOs in the capital city of Manila. My sponsors were grateful that I agreed to headline their event on such short notice that they presented me with a weekend getaway to one of their plush island resorts.

The area was called Palawan. The resort was named Club Paradise. To get there was an adventure that felt like it came straight out of an Indiana Jones movie. My girlfriend (from Manila) and I chartered a twin-engine airplane that sat four people. It was a really bumpy flight. Several times I felt like I was going to puke my guts out. The island was remote and desolate. We landed on an old dirt runway and what looked like a shack immediately came into view. There was a sign on the shack that read: Welcome to Club Paradise. We were allowed to go in and buy a soda and snacks. After a few minutes a jeep arrived. Our guide said, "Welcome to Club Paradise." We got into the jeep and for the next forty-five minutes bounced around like crazy through the mountains in the back seat. Then we came to a giant crater—it was as far as the jeep could go. From that point on, my girlfriend and I had to walk around the crater and then we followed our guide to this old bamboo walking bridge. As the bridge swayed gently from side to side, in a single file we crossed over some desolate land until we reached a river with an old small boat waiting there for us.

The two-person crew also said to us, "Welcome to Club Paradise." They handed us sandwiches and a Coke. They pushed the boat back and we started going upstream. After about twenty minutes, the river widened and transformed into this beautiful, dark blue ocean. It was a bit nerve-racking to be in this tiny boat in the heart of one of the deepest oceans I'd ever been on. However, the trip was absolutely breathtaking—some of the most beautiful scenery I have ever witnessed. Imagine, if you will, pristine blue water surrounded by large mountains on either side—unspoiled by mankind, just like you would see on a post card.

Up ahead in the distance we could see there was an island. We were headed right toward it. I asked the guide, "Is that Club Paradise?" He smiled and nodded his head up and down.

When we arrived the boat went right up on the beach. We were instructed to jump out and the crew once again said: "Welcome to Club Paradise." The water was crystal clear and the beaches were powdery white and extremely soft and gentle on the feet. It was like no other sand I had ever felt.

There were several dozen cottages sprawled out along the beach. They were decorated in a romantic tropical atmosphere—dreamlike. I was with a beautiful twenty-two-year-old brunette bombshell. You couldn't ask for anything else, except... there was no Internet or telephone service. I had no access to the outside world except if there was an emergency. I didn't know any of this until after I arrived. It was beautiful, but it drove me crazy.

How much relaxing can someone do? For the ultimate workaholic like me it was pure torture. I couldn't even exercise except walk on the beach, which I did. How pathetic is that? And it was just for the weekend. I always felt guilty if I missed work-related opportunities. It tore at my insides because I just knew I was missing something important.

This dreadful, nagging feeling came over me whether I was on vacation or not. I used to think about work while having dinner at a restaurant with my family or friends. I may have been smiling and joking around but my mind was back on my computer. I was a great actor—I faked it so well. For me, the ultimate workaholic, listening to that stupid babble while having dinner was a complete waste of time.

Control Freak

There's no such thing as teamwork—it's all about having full control. The politically correct term is teamwork. For me it was just a bunch of nonsense. I always believed that the only way to guarantee that the job was done right and ahead of schedule was to do it myself. So when it came down to completing projects with unrealistic deadlines, I could only count on myself to work around the clock to get the job done ahead of schedule, under budget, and well. It was all about me, myself and I meeting this objective.

I couldn't always depend on others to work around the clock to produce the way I did. In many situations it was easier to focus on it myself and not have to deal with co-workers. Yes, you might say I was the *MicroManager from Hell*. I didn't like to delegate until I was 100 percent sure the right team was in place, and every member was willing to work with a sense of urgency like I always did. Most workaholics don't like to delegate. They're always afraid of others making mistakes that could impact their deliverables. Sharing the workload is simply not in their vocabulary.

Hooked on Mobile Devices (For Work Only)

Day or night and in any kind of weather, I was always looking at email on my handheld device. I never played games on it, listened to music or even surfed the Web. It was strictly for work. It didn't matter where I happened to be or what I was doing. Even when I had an evening business appointment or a date, I was always checking my email. I did it all the time, even in the bathroom—heck, even when I was intimate with a woman. The moment I was done climaxing I would grab for my device and forget about the naked person next to me. Once again, I admit this was pretty pathetic behavior on my part. What can I say, workaholism turned me into one sick *hombre*.

Stress and the Workaholic

Too much work—even for the ultimate workaholic? There were times when I've taken on too much that it wore me down both physically and mentally, but I was much too proud to show any signs of fatigue. Heaven forbid if I showed symptoms of being human, at least in public any way. One evening there was a major software upgrade to our manufacturing systems, which were critical for our quarter-end revenue posting. I had already worked most of the night to oversee the upgrade, which went fairly smoothly. By 9 A.M. there was a line outside my office stretching around the hall to run special requests against the upgraded systems.

I was already wasted from the ungodly number of hours invested the previous night. My patience was wearing thin. I was stressed beyond belief. However La Machine had to remain calm, cool and collected. I couldn't show any signs of weakness. All I wanted was to make a quick getaway, but it would have been a suicidal career move. So I excused myself for five minutes, took refuge inside the restroom, and splashed cold water on my face. Once I managed to regain my composure, I headed right back to my office with a renewed fortitude to take on that line of demanding users.

Impatient to the Bone

I used to be impatient with everyone except management. Unless you were someone helping me excel in my career there was no time for idle chitchat. I always found a way to politely cut off conversations as quickly as possible and get back to thinking about my next task or project. The same was true in my personal life. I was especially impatient with people who were too detail-oriented and babbled needlessly. In my view, chatting solely for the sake of making conversation was a waste of valuable resources. Communication was cut off immediately in the appropriate manner. I wasn't rude by any means, but I *always* cut babblers off—in a nice way of course.

Family members and their drama also took a back seat to my career. A family member bitching about this or that simply did not benefit my career in any way, shape, or form. That being the case, what they said to me went in one ear and out the other. Even though I was looking straight at them, the truth is I was tuning them out the whole time. Whether I was having dinner with friends, family or my wife the conversation always gravitated towards work. All I wanted to talk about was a new work-related project, future corporate travel plans, and heated office politics; basically, I had nothing else to say because I was out of touch with reality and everyone around me.

The Memory of a Sieve

Back then one of my greatest faults was that I had the memory of a sieve. More times than I care to admit, I would forget that it was my night to pick up my son from soccer practice or that I had promised my wife to be home by 6:00 P.M. for dinner and I would show up two hours late. I was constantly forgetting things that weren't associated with my job. To make matters worse, I also forgot important birthdays, anniversaries and other special events. My undivided attention was always focused on work projects. I used to tell people jokingly (but deep down I wasn't joking) that if something wasn't associated with my two priorities it would probably fall through the cracks.

Power is King

Who doesn't love the feeling of power? I could never have enough. It was a major adrenalin rush. I wanted to be king of the hill—to rule in a manner that commanded respect from my kingdom. I was respected throughout the company and had a reputation for getting the job done, not just in Mike's department. The executive and leadership team knew my name and I was requested to speak at technology and success events all over the world. I wasn't obnoxious—my accomplishments and credibility spoke for itself. My colleagues witnessed me authoring and publishing several dozen books with Prentice Hall, an imprint of one of the largest publishing companies in the world, while I was a Vice-President in a multi-billion dollar company. In comparison to others, I had a biography that was second to none. It was full of outstanding accomplishments and I knew it. That's the way I planned it. The sales and marketing divisions in the company actually leveraged my name to boost revenue.

In the dot-com era, wearing casual attire was in, especially at our company. Our CEO used to wear jeans to work. I was tall, easy on the eyes, and fit nicely into my jeans. At least that's what people have always told me. I was and still am physically fit. It's taken me years of exercising religiously to develop a well-sculpted chest, arms, and shoulders. Whenever I was speaking I knew that the audience was checking out my physique as well as listening to what I had to say and this inflated my ego even more.

In retrospect, the ugly part of wielding such power was that I purposely misused it just for the sake of having more fun at the expense of others. It was easy picking. Everyone practically worshipped the ground I walked on and respected me for my intelligence, discipline, and accomplishments. Taking advantage of whoever I wanted was like child's play. I'm not proud of my actions; being so arrogant—all that power truly got to my head.

The way I lived life made perfect sense to me. I was making tons of money, traveling the world over as an international motivational speaker, meeting beautiful women left and right. Who in their right mind wouldn't want this kind of lifestyle? Everything I did produced great results and turned me on in a big way. When I had a new idea, people stopped what they were doing and listened. If they didn't like it in the end, I could care less. It was my way or the highway.

It's a known fact that people will always gravitate toward successful individuals. If you're a person with low self-esteem to begin with and you may not necessarily have the best social skills, then being a successful businessman is a good thing. You begin feeling more secure because for the first time people are respectful of your success and stature. They are listening to you. The tides have turned and the harder you work, the more successful you become. You love the attention and it's making you work harder than ever before.

Lucky for me, I had the gift of gab. I also played the corporate politics game rather well. I have always referred to this as a game because in my opinion following bogus company protocol is so stupid and such a waste of resources. Unfortunately, it is a necessary evil and if you don't play along chances are you will never survive in today's fast-paced and cutthroat corporate world. I could say anything to get what I wanted to accomplish my work-related goals and it didn't matter who I stepped on to make that happen. Yeah, I was ruthless.

When you have crossed the line from being a hard worker to an extremist workaholic, sooner than later everything else in your life becomes secondary. The person you have become is not the one God intended you to be. But you don't care because all of this attention feels great. You wouldn't have it any other way until the day it all comes crashing down and you've got nothing but misty water-colored memories to keep you warm at night.

Story: The Corporate Affair with Indirect Report

I was in my late thirties and Anne (fictitious name), a very sexy blonde, was in her late twenties. At the time I was married and so was she. She used to work the later shift from 3 P.M.-11 P.M. in the Data Center. Whenever I wanted to take a break, I would go into the Data Center and shoot the breeze with the gang—probably once or twice a week. The Data Center was where my career had started twenty years earlier. It was fun for the staff and it also gave me a breather from my intense work activities.

As much as I hate to admit it, there was also an ulterior motive for my regular visits to the Data Center. I was actually getting to know Anne better each time I walked in there. She was already impressed by me and I could tell she was always checking me out when I was talking with some of the guys. There were typically two to three people working each shift depending on which night of the week it was. On this particular evening, to my amazement, only Anne was working. When I asked her where the other co-worker was, she said he had called in sick.

There she was, wearing a beautiful red dress. So, I asked her why she was all dressed up. Anne said it was her birthday and she felt like going out afterward. Naturally, I said, "Happy birthday and have a blast after work," then I said, "Good night" as I usually do.

Right before walking out the room, Anne surprisingly popped the million dollar question, "Aren't you going to buy me a birthday drink?"

"I'm sorry. Sure let's get a drink when you get off of work."

When Anne got off, I followed her to the bar at the Hyatt hotel a few miles down the road. We walked in together as if we were co-workers. After she had a few drinks we walked out as a couple. When we got back to her car we made out for a while. A few nights later we got a room at a different hotel and my first corporate affair was in full swing. Anne and I lasted a few months before she got another job. Not something to be proud of, but I felt invincible, so why not? Other affairs followed, at least a dozen in the corporate world.

Story: Corporate Affair with Direct Report

This indiscretion was the ultimate in cockiness and stupidity. How stupid could I be? In my defense, she was smoking hot and I was invincible—right? The power I had over people got to my head. One of my direct reports used to wear these tight jeans that made her look awesome. She had one of the greatest butts I had ever seen. She was intelligent, resourceful, and a hard worker. Oh, did I mention that she was also very married? She was also a high-maintenance type of employee with many personal issues. There was always some sort of drama going on in her life.

I decided that I had to have that ass of hers. It was driving me crazy. We had weekly one-on-one meetings, which I facilitated in my office. It was always legitimate without any hidden agendas. But the next meeting was going to be different. After we went over our typical agenda items, I mentioned that I was really hungry and suggested we continue our discussion over lunch. She happily agreed. While at lunch I told her that I liked her. She was blown away. She asked: "Aren't you married?"

I answered, "Yes." Then I asked if I made her nervous.

"A bit."

At this point, I asked her if she wanted to go to the park just to sit there and talk. Amazingly, she agreed.

I knew she liked wine so I asked her if we should stop by and get some. She indicated to me that it was a good idea: "I could use some right about now."

While at the park I started kissing her and she didn't resist. I asked her if she wanted to go somewhere to finish drinking this. Within fifteen minutes we were in a hotel room. I finally got what I wanted, but from that point forward her personal issues and the drama that followed had me worried—she could say something to HR and ruin my career. Luckily she never did.

Other Corporate Indiscretions
Story: The Nineteen-Year-Old Blonde Bombshell

She was from a small farming town in Ohio and drove to California to fulfill her dream of working in the Information Technology industry in Silicon Valley. This young woman was intelligent and beautiful—she also had a lot of *chutzpah* to make that trip by herself. I actually hired her because she was disciplined. You could tell she was driven to succeed at all costs. Not long after I hired her, she immediately made an impact on the organization. Her performance was excellent. She consistently produced quality deliverables ahead of schedule. She may have been young, but she handled herself like a seasoned pro.

At that time, I was in my early thirties, running a global IT department with approximately sixty-five employees for a major Japanese company. My new hire turned heads wherever she went, with her long, naturally curly blonde hair and curvy figure. A real sight to behold! Her beauty caught my attention as well. I fought the urges for the longest time due to the risks involved, but in the end my ugly workaholic mannerisms coupled with an insatiable ego won over any morals I had. Although she had a fiancé—a pilot in the Air Force back home in Ohio—I wanted to nail her. The hunt began. For months, I befriended her nonchalantly, striking up conversations whenever possible. She had no clue I had ulterior motives and neither did the rest of the department. That's how good I was at the seduction game.

After about six months of working for the company, she requested a week off to work from home for personal reasons and her supervisor obliged. Although she was taking time off, she still wanted to connect to our corporate computers and work. To do this, she needed to take home a monitor, keyboard and modem to be able to connect to our main systems. She requested the equipment through her supervisor, but it wasn't ready to go out on her last day before starting her sabbatical. Her supervisor said that he would contact her once the equipment was available. I told the supervisor to let me know when the equipment was ready as well—her apartment was on my way home and I could drop it off. He didn't suspect a thing... This was a one-way ticket "in," if you catch my drift.

When the equipment was ready I called her up and told her that I was going to drop it off on the way home. She was surprised to hear from me, but grateful—it saved her a separate trip into the office. Once I got to her apartment, I rang the doorbell and within seconds she answered and asked me to come in. I told her that the equipment was in my car and that we should probably remove it right away. Once we retrieved it, I suggested, "I should probably help you set it up—this technology can be problematic." Of course this was a line of BS. To seal the deal, I also told her, "Telecommunications and setting up remote locations to communicate with corporate are two of my areas of expertise. I did it full-time before getting into management." (Another line of BS.)

She said, "Great! I would sincerely appreciate it."

We set it all up and tested the equipment in her bedroom—all worked as advertised. She was happy. She offered me a Diet Coke and we sat on the couch and talked for a while. That's when the BS came on thick and heavy. I went straight for the jugular. I told her how much I admired her tenacity and determination, that she was beautiful and sexy, that I thought we should go out.

Shortly thereafter, I was between her legs and enjoying every minute of it. I never finished that Diet Coke. Reflecting back, she was the sweetest girl and I manipulated her emotions for the longest time to meet my selfish needs, just to accomplish another goal. Once I got bored, I went on to my next conquest.

Story: The Bubbly Payroll Clerk in the Adjacent Department
She was in her mid-twenties—always smiling with a bubbly and outgoing personality. She was definitely the flirtatious type. So

naturally when the timing was right, I flirted back. She was petite, cute with a nice body to feed my hungry ego and appetite for fresh meat. There was very little effort involved in closing the deal—we actually *did it* in the back room of the data center one day. We had several encounters in the same back office, right on top of the desk. Sure it was risky, but as the ultimate workaholic, I felt invincible. This continued for a few months until I was tired of the intimacy. But I enjoyed communicating with her. I introduced her to my best friend at the time. This was over three decades ago and they're still married.

Story: The Exotic-Looking Accounting Manager

This woman was a real stunner and carried herself well, showcasing her long straight black hair and large brown eyes. She would always wear business suits and dresses—she looked awesome in them.

I passed by her department several times a week just to catch a glimpse of her beauty. I would always smile and say hi and she would return the gesture. Whenever our paths crossed in the hallway I would strike up longer conversations. One day, out of the blue, I told her that she was gorgeous and I wanted to have lunch with her.

She said, "Aren't you married?"

I replied, "Yes, and so are you."

We went to lunch and clicked right away. I kept staring into her big brown eyes while she was talking and we both felt the vibes between us. After lunch I thanked her and we went our separate ways. I let her stew on things for a few days—purposely avoiding her.

The following week, I went in for the kill. I asked her if she wanted to meet for a few snacks at the local eatery after work. We went there and we had a good time, just talking and laughing. When we left I walked her to her car—except it wasn't a car. It was her family's mobile home; her car was in the shop.

I said to her, "Wow, very nice! I've never been in one of these" (one of my signature BS lines).

She asked if I wanted to see the inside.

Casually, I replied "Sure."

I went in and as soon as she closed the door I put her in my arms and looked into her eyes and kissed her big-time. Then I put my hands up her dress and everything started coming off.

Obsessed with Money

Pretty women were not the only thing I liked. I also loved expensive toys. I honestly felt I deserved the best of everything—the more, the better. Why not? I worked my ass off after all. As the ultimate workaholic, I possessed a *never enough mentality*. The harder I worked, the more money I made. In my mind, more money equated to extra toys. It was a status symbol. I wanted to look and act the part of the high-rolling executive. Due to my sense of entitlement, I simply had to have the most expensive suits and drive that fancy black Mercedes. But not just any Mercedes, only the top of the line was going to appease me. It was a brand new 2000 SL500, black-on-black with beautiful, shiny chrome rims (AMX package). Did I really need it? Hell no—it was just to feed my stupid ego.

At this juncture in my life, I had everything a man could ever ask for: money, stature, fancy cars, speed boat, major accomplishments, a nice physique, good looks, and a good personality to boot. I was the ultimate, happy workaholic. How could anybody claim there was something wrong with the way I was living? I was 100 percent convinced that I needed to keep on focusing on my career and health and everything else would just have to take a back seat. It was all about the Harris Kern brand. I took a path where the only thing that mattered was the more money I earned, the more power I possessed, the bigger the ego, and the happier I became. It was a pretty sick game I played... but extremely common behavior for the ultimate workaholic.

Story: Money and Me, a Marriage Made in Hell

My love affair with money started when I was 13 years old, the day of my *bar mitzvah*. It was a few hours after the formal ceremony in the Temple when my family, the congregation and I all headed to a large building several miles away, which my parents had rented to celebrate my manhood. We got there before the congregation and formed a line in the hallway leading into a big ballroom. I remember standing in line greeting everyone. As I was shaking hands, many of the men would give me an envelope in the other hand.

That evening when I opened those envelopes, my life changed. I would never be the same again. There must have been at least twenty envelopes. Each one contained some form of money (cash, checks, bonds). Sure, I got other gifts too: the usual fancy pens, wallets and organizers. But nothing excited me more than the money. The more envelopes I opened, the larger my eyes grew and the seed of greed was planted in my heart, right then and there.

This was a pivotal moment in my life when my obsession for more money first began. I put every dollar in the bank. That's what my parents told me to do. They advised me, "Make it grow. Do not spend it. We provide you with food, a home and clothing. Don't buy music paraphernalia, little knickknacks at the mall or waste your money on food with your friends—even though we give you an allowance for incidentals. You should deposit your allowance money in the bank, too. You will need to buy a car and a home one day." *Earn more, save more, and spend nothing* was their motto, which has stuck with me my whole life.

As the years went by, my lust for money only got worse. I was always working multiple jobs: mowing lawns, delivering newspapers on my bicycle, or helping my neighbor file travel brochures at his travel agency on the weekends. Just about every dollar I made went into the bank. Watching the numbers grow was a major turn-on for me. As I got older and started working in the corporate world, the bigger the paycheck, the larger the dollar signs in my eyes became. The larger the bonus I received, the harder I worked the following year to get an even bigger one with more stock options. No matter how fat my wallet got, it was never enough for me.

What Personal Life?

Forget it! For most workaholics their personal life is minimal or it didn't exist—period. But that's of very little consequence to them. At the end of the day, there's little energy to invest into their personal life any way. In general, workaholics don't have many friends, activities or hobbies. Their exaggerated work habits either put a damper or totally ruined their personal relationships. For most of them, maintaining personal relationships just isn't a priority, it certainly wasn't with me. Of course, I still had physical needs, but I found a way to fulfill those desires for intimacy without committing to a relationship that gobbled up a lot of my time and resources.

The way I viewed it, I just didn't have the time to deal with drama. Dealing with human emotions, especially those of the female persuasion, was a total time waster. I tried to avoid it like I was avoiding Ebola. When most people get stressed out about something in their personal life, they want to address it as quickly as possible, confront the issue and resolve the conflict before it escalates even further. Others think that the best course of action is to get away for a few days, especially if there is a sensitive issue with their spouse. They try to flee from the situation at hand altogether and attempt to have some fun with the hope it will miraculously resolve the problem as quickly as possible. The workaholic takes this second strategy. When a sensitive issue in their personal life rears its ugly head, they much prefer to ignore it, hoping that the issue mysteriously disappears.

That's what I did all the time. Work was my outlet and security blanket. I had very little patience for personal issues. When I had to deal with them, I detested it and always looked for ways out of the situation quickly or I would just bury my head in my work like an ostrich buries theirs in the sand.

Ignored Quality Family Time

As much as it pains me to admit it, I neglected to spend quality time with my family. The few times I did spend with my children, I pretty much improvised. Although I spent time with them, it wasn't really *quality* time. I might have been there with them physically, but my mind was always floating around elsewhere. After my first wife and I divorced, I would pick up my son after school and take him back to the hotel where I would always stay. My son loved it there. It was a typical four-star hotel with all the amenities and as a frequent traveler, I would always have access to the concierge lounge where they had a large and very nice sitting area with several TVs and great food. I would bring my son in there so he could watch his favorite TV shows to keep him occupied so I could do my work. Instead of interacting with my son like any good father would, I took care of my selfish needs. As I look back now, I could kick myself in the butt. There are no second chances for several things in life.

"I'm Busy" Was My Middle Name

I used the phrase "I'm busy" so much that it could have easily been my middle name. I wielded these two words as skillfully as any samurai handles his sword, whether it was to get out of going to a doctor's appointment my wife had made for me, a holiday get-together with family or a wedding, all of which I hated anyway. Those infamous words got me out of just about everything. I had a knack for making it sound like there was an all-out crisis at the office that needed my immediate attention. When my wife wanted attention, I didn't give it to her because I was preoccupied with work day and night. This was so asinine on my part. She was only trying to keep me healthy and I wouldn't listen. The doctor appointments were for my own good, yet I still wouldn't listen. It was Harris' own little world and there was no room for anyone else in it.

No Consideration for Significant Others

Intimate moments with your significant other are typically very special, or at least they should be. For me, not so much. I wanted the sex, that's for sure. But I did not want the drama that came along with it, especially—to be real blunt here—after they had climaxed. I remember on many occasions, as soon as I was done pleasing my partner, I made excuses to leave. I wanted to get back to work or just go to sleep so I could get to the gym and work early in the morning. Yeah, I know it sounds horrible and pretty pathetic. It doesn't get much worse than this, but it was the truth back then. The minute I took care of my physical desires, all I wanted to do was get back to my mental stimulation.

No Morals—One Sick M.F.

What morals? I had none. They had been thrown out the window a long time ago. While I never broke the law, looking back and reflecting on all the horrible things I did to people were just as bad as I had done something illegal—if not worse. It was nothing about being a good person—it all boiled down to being successful and having a *whatever-it-takes* attitude. Many workaholics lose their morals early on in their career. They take whatever actions necessary to get the job done. Once they become successful and beaming with confidence morals are no longer part of the equation. I was the worst. I thought I could get away with anything—guess again, Mr. Kern.

Story: A Sick Record—Yet, I was Proud of it

While writing this book, I turned sixty years old. As I dwell for a moment on how truly selfish I was... well, two words come to mind: *downright sickening*. This pretty much depicts a large part of my life living with this wicked disease I call workaholism.

As mentioned before, I managed to make excuses for never going to weddings, anniversary parties, funerals or *bar mitzvahs* held for any family member. Stop and think about that for a moment. I had an average-sized family with aunts and uncles spread throughout the states. There were always family functions, celebrations, events, tragic ceremonies—yet, I would always play my *I'm too busy* card to justify not leaving work. **Not even for a funeral** to pay my last respects to a family member I had known most of my life. They attended my *bar mitzvah* and were supportive at my high school graduation. This family gave me gifts, thought of me as one of their own, and were concerned about my happiness, but where was I for them? I didn't have the heart or good sense to do something for them as simple as attend a funeral to mourn the loss of their loved one. I used to tout this *sick and ugly* record because of the time I saved and was able to invest in my work. Now I'm ashamed to even write this section.

Ray was a childhood friend throughout middle school and high school. We would hang out together, as time permitted. When the gang used to go to the lake together, I made sure Ray came along. He was a really nice guy, but had issues—he was emotionally challenged. His mom would always ask me to watch over him and I did. I kept him safe and out of trouble. His mom was forever grateful to me for helping her with Ray. She would cook up a storm for us all the time. She was a super nice lady. Over time, I drifted away as my workaholism took a hold of my morals and any common sense I had. I'll never forget the day I received a call from Ray's mom. She was crying as she told me Ray had committed suicide. I found out that he had blown his brains out with a shotgun. She asked me to please be at her son's funeral. It was all she wanted. Ray would have wanted that too. I said yes—but never showed up. This was f***ed up.

There was one funeral I did go to, but ONLY because it was work-related and the politically correct thing to do. I was truly a piece of work. My boss requested that I go, otherwise I wouldn't have, although a good friend and great human being just died unexpectedly. It was for someone I had known for more than twenty years. He was my former boss and a friend of mine. I actually got him hired at our company and he was killed in a shooting incident—a drive-by shooting on the freeway.

When I attended the funeral, his wife actually thanked me for getting Larry the job. She said he was always praising me for that. And I hadn't been going to attend his funeral in the first place. You have no idea how low I felt.

Story: The Puerto Rican Goddess and the Ultimate Workaholic

Writing this section was *extremely* hard for me. My Puerto Rican Goddess, who left me a few years ago has turned my life upside down. Up until then, I never cried in my life. I didn't know how. Besides, machines don't cry—right? This one-time heap of metal was reduced to a pile of rusty old bolts. There are times I still cry like a baby. I now live alone in our big and empty six-bedroom monster home in a suburb of Dallas, Texas. I have all the wedding pictures up on the walls, captured images from our travels and romantic cards from special occasions. It looks like she's home with our children, but it's only me, that stupid workaholic, who is home alone.

I was and still am waiting for my wife Mayra to come back into my arms. I'm fully prepared to wait for the rest of my life if I have to. I hold one of our wedding pictures and the Holy Bible in my hand, as I lie down on top of my sleeping bag, before saying my prayers and falling asleep. Yes, that's not a typo. I sleep on a sleeping bag. Even though I have access to a beautiful king-sized brass bed, I have vowed to never sleep in what was our matrimonial bed for many years without my wife. The only exception to this rule is if I am dying. Then I would sprawl out on my side of the bed, because that's where I'd want her to find me.

Long after this book hits the shelves, I will only sleep with my Puerto Rican Goddess in *our* bed. Regardless of the pain of reliving this nightmare over and over again, it's my destiny to die like this, with her in my heart, soul and mind. There isn't a day or an hour that goes by that I don't think about my love. She was and still is my everything. I love her dearly.

She's extremely talented—the creative type. A good artist, writer, and graphics designer. She just never applied herself. But I married Mayra for her heart and not for her initiative. I am waiting for her return—not because of her beauty or heart, but because *she deserves the best and I know I am second to none in all categories.* I am not being egotistical here. What I'm saying is that I am merely confident of all the things I'm capable of accomplishing. I have made some horrible mistakes in my life, but I have learned from them and am striving every day to correct my wrongdoings. If she is as strong a Christian as she has always claimed to be who forgives, then she will come back to me. If not, that is God's will.

Despite her absence, Mayra still continues to be my everything. She was and still is my best friend, business partner, confidant, lover and wife. I used to call her Cleopatra because she looked just like Elizabeth Taylor in her portrayal of Cleopatra. She used to style her hair in the same way. I idolize her—I actually put her on a pedestal, mostly because of her beautiful heart. Her physical beauty is just the icing on the cake. In hindsight, I have known hundreds of beautiful women, but her beauty is as much internal as external. Actually, it's much more internal—she truly has a heart of gold.

In 2000, I met Mayra Muniz, a front desk manager at the Barbizon Hotel in New York City. I used to travel frequently to Manhattan on business, but always stayed at the former Marriott Hotel at the World Trade Center prior to 9/11. One day a friend of mine told me to stay at the Barbizon because it was physically attached and associated with one of the best gyms in Manhattan— The Equinox.

I met Mayra during one of my first stays at the Barbizon, she checked me in at the front desk. She was beautiful and in her early thirties. That day her hair was a bit messy. It was long and curly— you could tell it took her a lot of time to maintain it. That particular morning she didn't have time to fix it. I was easily fifteen years her senior. When she opened her mouth and spoke to me, I knew I wanted to have this woman. I wanted to meet her socially, so I made it a goal.

The next day I put my plan into motion. After my workout, I went by the front desk to say good morning to her, but only for a minute—she was busy. I went upstairs and got ready for work. Before going to work, I called the front desk and Mayra answered the phone. I put in a request for ten large FedEx boxes.

She asked, "Ten?"

"Yes—please. I need to ship out some books."

"Okay, they will be in your room later this afternoon."

I didn't really need ten boxes, but I wanted to make an impression and stand out from the rest of the businessmen who were constantly trying to hit on her. I could only imagine.

The next morning, after my workout, I purchased my protein drink and bought one for her too—to say thank you for the boxes. She loved the drink, so I continued to buy her one daily for the next several weeks.

Her personality and beauty always intimidated me. I was always shy around her. Just about every morning I would stand and hide behind the wall of the front lobby and take a peek at her while she was working. I had no idea but she finally told me that she knew I was doing that, but thought it was cute. I finally got the nerve to ask her out for dinner. She agreed.

It was the most memorable night of my life. It was a cold wintery evening in Manhattan—in the thirties. We met on the west side for coffee and cheesecake instead of dinner. Then we just talked and walked for the next four hours from the west side of Manhattan to the east side. In total, I'd say it was probably fifty blocks—but who was counting? We were just holding hands and talking. Occasionally, I would put my arm around her. I thoroughly enjoyed our walk and lengthy conversation.

She had some major issues to deal with. It turned out that she was a single mom with two children by two deadbeat dads. She was the only one supporting her son Christian and daughter Chade. Mayra went on to tell me she was in debt (credit card and student loans). At this juncture, most men would have headed straight for the nearest EXIT sign. Nobody wants that type of baggage—except me. I actually wanted to help her and the kids—not out of pity, but because I adored this woman. After four months, I asked her to marry me and she accepted. I had the woman I wanted for the rest of my life.

I took her all over the world with me: Hawaii, Las Vegas, Hong Kong, Australia (several times), Singapore, Amsterdam, and other great places. SO many great memories and SO much fun. Then I went back to my old workaholic ways and put my Goddess and Christian and Chade on the back burner. To make a long story shorter—fifteen years later, Mayra ended up leaving me, but it was the awakening I needed. She thought I was seeing someone else, but I never cheated on her with any person. I cheated on her with my workaholic mannerisms, by taking time away from our relationship. It wasn't Mayra's fault—it was all mine.

In the end, I lost Mayra and the children. My biggest fear came to fruition. I was alone. Mayra and I still speak to one another and are relatively close. I am hopeful she will give me another chance. If she doesn't, I am destined to die with only her in my heart. Although I consider myself a good catch for any woman, I will not get into another relationship. I only want to die with Mayra in my heart. I will only love HER for the rest of my existence. All I can do is keep praying day and night and never go back on my morals.

Summarizing the Bad and Ugly Characteristics

Do you possess some of those horrific traits or are you slowly gravitating toward being the person I've just described? Maybe you don't have all of those bad characteristics, but even a handful could really impact your life in a negative way. Nobody wants to go there. Listen to someone who was once the happiest workaholic of them all. Life is too short and if you don't heed my warning, you will fall, and fall hard, like I did.

It's not a pretty picture to paint of anyone, but workaholics won't disagree. They just shrug it all off and continue down that same "disaster-lurking-ahead" path until they take that hard fall. I was bad and the things I did were ugly. Did I break the law? Nope, I was too smart to throw my life away for not obeying the law, but in hindsight everything I did was worse than doing something that would land me behind bars. I hurt so many people—probably thousands. I'm truly amazed that God has kept me alive this long. A part of me would like to think the reason He has done that is so I can share my stories with others and continue to mentor people to follow their faith and maintain balance by being disciplined.

I would consider all of the symptoms identified in this chapter the voluntary type. Nobody put a gun to my head to behave in that manner. I chose that lifestyle. Initially, I didn't think there was anything wrong with being a workaholic. The benefits (listed below) outweighed the negatives:

- Accelerated career advancement
- Increased income (typically higher salaries and bonuses)
- Increased confidence with professional capabilities
- Accelerated growth in knowledge base
- Superior performance
- Continuous drive
- Constant productivity
- High efficiency
- Living a structured lifestyle

At the time the benefits kept on giving and it turned me on. They kept on paying big dividends. It was truly exhilarating. The feeling of accomplishment was never-ending. It lasted a *long* time and with over forty books published—the royalties were a gift that kept on giving. However, if you keep burning the candle around the clock, eventually something severe will take you down. If you throw in some common sense and focus equally in other key areas of your life, like health and important relationships in the long run, you will be a happier person and have a better quality of life.

CHAPTER FIVE

Roadmap to a Balanced Life

As a workaholic, you know how to design a strategy to become successful in your professional world. For large projects, you develop a roadmap with tasks, owners, key milestones, and deliverable dates. You have no problem holding yourself accountable to complete deliverables ahead of schedule. It has all become second nature to you as you've been doing this for years. This mode of operation has probably been instrumental in getting you to the top of the corporate ladder.

Now take that same or rather similar *structured* approach you've used in the corporate world for years and apply it to your personal life. It's not rocket science, but it does take a concerted effort on your part. Invest the time to thoroughly plan and then develop a roadmap to help you take the proper path for success. Planning and developing a roadmap is merely one aspect. Holding yourself accountable and *seriously* managing your life is a whole different ballgame.

The project you will be working on now is called managing a balanced life—it is life-altering. It is also likely to be the toughest challenge you've ever faced. If you fail, you stand to lose everything you've acquired to date. Make no mistake: your focus will be tested like never before. Instead of focusing on one priority, you will need to concentrate on all three major priorities: career, health, and relationships. For me it was a formidable challenge, but I took it on like I did every other challenge that came my way. It begins with a strategy.

Design a New Strategy

Being a workaholic means you're goal-oriented and accomplishment-motivated. On a constant basis, you're on top of the world and it feels great to you. Bring on more to divide and conquer and you will accomplish more. Let's face it: you're an addict. The more work gets piled on your plate, the more invincible you feel. This is your reality. No amount of work, accomplishments, and success shall ever be enough to satisfy the hunger in you. No one knows what a great feeling being a workaholic is better than me. Clearly, I'm not suggesting that you slow down. I know that won't work. But what I am recommending is that you modify your mode of operation to include a few new priorities.

So-called specialists can pontificate all they want by telling you to relax and smell the roses before something devastating happens to you, but who are they to tell you anything? You're highly accomplished. Why on earth would you stop and listen to anyone, especially if you're blazing your own trail? If I were you—as I was at one point not so long ago—I would be highly skeptical about taking this course of action. It may not seem like it now, but there is a dosage of sanity and some truth in what these self-proclaimed addiction specialists are preaching. However, telling you to relax alone will not work. Trying would only stress you out even more. Telling you to stop and smell the roses is just a big waste of their time and breath—you're not going to do that. Surprisingly, the right piece of advice to offer you is to accomplish more. That's right. I want you to accomplish more by focusing on your personal life as much as you do on your professional world. I, Harris Kern, want you to accomplish so much that you leave behind a legacy with your work-related achievements and in your personal space. That's what life is all about. Leave that legacy behind for your family. Don't just leave.

By making the necessary adjustments, you will wake up with a purpose and continue to look forward to accomplishing something major every day, just like you always have, only now you'll do it knowing you are not neglecting the other important areas of your life. A truly meaningful life is all about waking up with a clear, defined purpose. But the crux of the matter is it's going to be difficult to introduce any sort of change in your life. The goal is to institute balance one step at a time. Begin by taking a snapshot of where you are today and where you want to end up in your career, with your health and in your personal relationships.

Harris's Strengths and Weaknesses

The first step in making these changes is to *thoroughly* understand your strengths and weaknesses. It's important to take a snapshot before proceeding any further. You need to know where you stand. Once you've acknowledged your weaknesses, you will know which areas to focus on and how much effort will be involved. Once you design a strategy and roadmap, *execute* like your life depends on it, at least the quality of it anyway. Once you've identified your weaknesses, let them sit and simmer for a day then come back and reread them—see if you've left any off the list. It's crucial to get an accurate picture.

It's rather simple to do. You know what you excel at and are aware of where you need improvement. Be very objective and truthful. This is your life—be honest. Below were my strengths and weaknesses before I took that hard fall:

Harris's Strengths	Harris's Weaknesses
Self-motivated	Poor in management of personal relationships, with little to no effort invested
Goal-oriented	Treating God as just a three-letter word
Extremely efficient with time	Egotistical
Structured: organized and punctual, with a routine and to-do list	Selfish
Intelligent	Money-hungry—everything is irrelevant unless it helps the bottom line
Solutions-oriented	Controlling, only trusting oneself to get the job done quickly and well
Regular in exercise, seven days a week	Impatient, especially with people who are detail-oriented
Career-oriented	Poor at listening
Abstinent from drinking, smoking, and drugs	
Urgent in life management	
Genuine	
Legacy-minded	
Highly accomplished	
Willing to do whatever it takes to get the job done	
Very confident in abilities	
Good manager of limited resources	
Good at bringing conversations to a close	
Afraid to death of failure (as a motivator)	
Optimal at managing sleep	
Dedicated	

As you can see in the Table above, during the peak of my workaholic lifestyle the strengths overshadowed the negatives by almost double. So, how can anyone tell you that being a workaholic is a dangerous disease? The same guy who lost just about everything because he didn't address his weaknesses, that's who. Trust me when I say you can no longer ignore your personal life—period.

Overview of Evaluation

If I were to summarize my strengths and weaknesses, I would have to say that I had excellent self-discipline skills: I was good at managing time and goals, efficient, focused, self-motivated, structured, and driven to a fault. However, all of my skills were directed to only two areas: my career and health. Initially, that sounded pretty darn good. But if you look further, you will see the real ugly side of me (the old Harris Kern). It was all about me and no one else. No one else mattered, not my friends, wife, children, or parents. Yes indeed, that was the despicable me.

On the Road to Redemption

Since then, I've addressed all of my weaknesses and now I make sure that I maintain balance every day of the year by including personal obligations, tasks and projects on my to-do list. I also follow a daily routine that encompasses the three major priorities in my life. For example, just recently my to-do list included a note to call my daughter, send my son a birthday card, wash my truck, say my prayers, and of course a host of work-related items. Do I still have weaknesses? Sure I do! Nobody's perfect.

Patience: I don't want to shut off my sense of urgency to accomplish things before their actual due date. I will never change the need to accomplish more in less time. I believe that having a sense of urgency should be the norm. Life is too short. You blink and ten years just whisked by. Don't just exist, live!

Dealing with babblers: Although I didn't mark it as a weakness, I still can't deal with people who babble too much or are too detail-oriented. Time is the most precious resource we have and I abhor wasting it. I always cut them off—politely, of course.

In retrospect, I've made tremendous progress and as long as all three priorities are featured and incorporated into my daily routine and on my to-do list, I will never revert back to my old ways of being a two priority man. The simple solution to remaining balanced is being structured, holding yourself accountable, and having the proper mindset to focus equally in all three critical areas of life. I will discuss the importance of structure later in this section.

Although my literary agent and sometime writing partner Leticia and I joke about me being a machine even at the age of 60, I have changed my ways to be more sensitive to human tendencies. Let's take a look at Leticia, who is very balanced.

Leticia's Strengths and Weaknesses

No two people are ever exactly alike. Leticia's strengths and weaknesses look much different than mine. She may have faults (who doesn't?), but she will probably never take that hard fall like I did. As long as she maintains her balance by keeping her faith and personal life in the forefront, Leticia will maintain that good quality of life she enjoys. Let's take a detailed look at all of her strengths and weaknesses and see why she will always be successful.

Leticia's Strengths	Leticia's Weaknesses
Intelligent	Poor time management: Doesn't manage all of her resources (time and energy) effectively. • Excessive babbling: With friends and colleagues • Doesn't know how to cut people off politely. • Too detail-oriented when speaking with executives
Creative	Lacks confidence in her abilities
Personable	Stresses easily
Sincere	Burns out quickly
Genuine	Has a small business mindset
Reliable	Lacks consistency in her exercise
Resourceful	Unstructured, eschewing a to-do list in favor of keeping everything in her head, resulting in constant, stressful clutter
Excellent communication skills	Resistant to change; doesn't strategize for improvement. She has a *business as usual* mentality.
Caring	
Gets the job done	
Productive	
Great writing skills	
Extremely knowledgeable about the publishing business	
Maintains a balanced lifestyle no matter what the circumstances, with equal focus on faith, family, and work	
Punctual	
Excellent parent and wife	
Dedicated	

I would hire her in a heartbeat—who wouldn't? There is no denying that she would be an excellent employee. Is she a leader? Not exactly, but she's a highly successful literary agent, acquisitions editor, and publisher of her very own imprint of books. But more importantly she is a genuinely happy individual.

Overview of Evaluation

What isn't articulated as you assess Leticia's strengths and weaknesses is her unwavering commitment as a mother, wife and business owner. She does a magnificent job of managing her life by maintaining balance regardless of daily work-related pressures. I know because we run a publishing business together. There's no question in my mind that if she focused all of her efforts on her work she could make a lot more money. However, she wouldn't be happy in the end.

An area where Leticia requires some *much* needed improvement is time management. She stresses and burns out easily because she's always running out of resources (time and energy). A big contributing factor is her excessive babbling. She is constantly in lengthy conversations, mostly because she just doesn't want to cut anyone off. She's always afraid of hurting someone's feelings. She needs to learn how to say no effectively. If she were more efficient managing her resources Leticia would more easily maintain her composure. In general her overall self-discipline skills need further development. Once she develops them, her confidence level and productivity will increase dramatically.

The Human

Just like everyone else eventually does, Leticia shuts down. She looks forward to vacations and getting her eight hours of sleep a night. On a regular basis, she needs time off to shut everything down and unwind with her glass of wine and two-hour baths. She likes to slow down and smell the roses as she hikes down the trails in the beautiful master-planned community of The Woodlands, Texas, the place she calls home. She is a magnificent human being and plays her role perfectly. She has the general quality of life we all desire.

I wouldn't want her lifestyle: she needs more breaks, more time to deal with personal issues, and more tender loving care (TLC).

She melts down under pressure frequently but even with all of her drama, she's still a keeper.

Has Progress Been Made?

Not really. Leticia still has poor self-discipline skills. It will take her years to break some of her bad habits—if she ever does. I say *if* because subconsciously she just doesn't grasp the need or urgency to fix these areas. She's also stubborn. Leticia has not made progress in key areas like excessive babbling. She's not cognizant of the time she wastes. She still doesn't value the most important and scarce commodity we have—time. She probably wastes a minimum of two hours a day on unnecessary babbling. She just won't change and although I've tried to coach her on my area of expertise, she doesn't listen.

Leticia needs to extrapolate the minutes she wastes babbling on any given day/week/month. It will be an eye-opening experience. Conference calls that she partakes in last twice as long as necessary. She will discuss unimportant topics that really do not need to be raised in these types of forums. She also doesn't strategize and prioritize work-related items effectively. As long as she has poor self-discipline skills, Leticia will never gain the confidence she so desperately seeks.

Balance

Everyone has heard that old cliché: *There's so much more to life than work*. Agreed, there is, but good luck trying to convince a happy workaholic of that. How do you convince someone that they need to have a more balanced lifestyle before it's too late and they take that hard fall like yours truly did? It doesn't take a rocket scientist to realize we all need balance to be happy and to improve our overall quality of life. Knowing it and doing something about it is as different as night and day. The workaholic is thriving in his or her career, which is the ultimate turn-on for them. What makes it even harder to change their mindset is that they are probably highly accomplished in their area of expertise.

Nowadays, I define living a balanced life as feeling happy, having peace of mind, being productive, waking up with a purpose and excelling at what you do. Simply stated, it's putting equal focus in the areas of your mental, physical, emotional, and spiritual well-being. Below are some examples of the benefits of having a balanced lifestyle and the risk of living an unbalanced one.

The Benefits of Living a Balanced Lifestyle	The Risk of Living an Unbalanced Life
Good mental, spiritual, emotional and physical health.	Putting all your eggs in one basket. Your strategy, energy and focus are on one area of your life. If things don't go according to plan, it could destroy you and you'll be left with nothing.
Improved personal life.	Failing in your personal relationships. You won't have the resources to invest quality time in friends or other special people in your life.
Enjoying vacations with your loved ones.	Probable painful divorce.
Improved quality of life by focusing on career, health and relationships equally.	Abandoning spirituality (always too busy).
Being in touch with God. Saying your prayers first thing each morning is a small obligation but a huge accomplishment, besides it feels great.	Loneliness and depression—burying your head further into your work when there are critical emotional issues to deal with. Your work becomes your only outlet.
Spending quality time with your son, daughter or someone special consistently—even if it's only one hour a day.	Living an unhealthy lifestyle.
Preventing some of the risks from occurring when focusing on only one priority.	
Reducing stress.	

It won't be easy to achieve a more balanced way of life, but it's doable. Compulsive work addiction takes time to develop and it will take considerable time to overcome. Just remember, the benefits of being balanced far outweigh the benefits of your current lifestyle.

Take the Balance Test if You Dare

Being proactive could very well save your life (marriage, family, career, soul, sanity, etc). How close or how far are you from having that balanced life everyone desires? Do you really know? I don't think so. I had no clue because I was always too busy with my career and exercise routine to do any kind of reality check. The first step is to know how bad your addictions really are—you need to know your numbers. You can't fix what you don't know. Once you assess how good or bad your numbers are, you can focus on making improvements.

Let's start with a simple evaluation, shall we? This evaluation should take approximately thirty minutes. That's not too much to utilize from your busy schedule. Dissect your life into the top three quadrants (priorities): career, health and relationships:

- Career (includes business, finances, education)
- Health (meal management, exercising consistently, and managing sleep optimally)
- Relationships (God, spouse, business colleagues, friends)

Now take a close look at your life. How much quality time are you spending in each area? Take the balance test below and determine the percentage of time you spend with each of the three priorities. There is no right answer or ideal breakdown. Everyone's situation is different. Go ahead and take the test. I'll wait.

Priority	Percentage of Time Spent	Steps for Improvement
Career		
Health • Meal management		
Health • Exercise		
Health • Managing sleep optimally		
Relationships • God		
Relationships • Spouse/Significant Other		
Relationships • Children		
Relationships • Business associates		
Relationships • Friends		

Perhaps in the career category you documented that you spend approximately 70 percent of your life on your job. Sometimes a high number is warranted. In most companies management throws many unrealistic demands at you all the time. You can't say no. You have no choices but to comply or risk getting that pink slip.

Under each of the top three priorities be as granular as possible. Under relationships, I broke it down into sub-categories. The same can be said about health. Your sub-categories could be different than mine, but the top three priorities should be the same. Once you've placed a percentage next to the appropriate category then determine next steps. What could you do differently to obtain that balanced lifestyle we all desire? Below is an example of the resources I allocated for my life, when I was the ultimate happy workaholic:

Priority	Percentage	Steps Needed For Improvement
Career	60%	Reduce the number of hours allocated for work in the evenings and weekends. Put a limit on it and try to do most of my work while the family is sleeping.
Health • Meal management	2.5%	No change—already a top priority.
Health • Exercise	10%	No change—already a top priority.
Health • Managing sleep optimally	2.5%	No change—already a top priority.
Relationships • God	0	Make God number one in my life. Include morning and evening prayers. Also include some type of daily devotional.
Relationships • Spouse/Significant Other	5%	Increase the time considerably and spend quality time together (date night, exercise together, take more walks holding hands, go for drives, watch more movies).
Relationships • Children	5%	Kids are older now and don't live at home but email, call and text them more frequently. Text and email a minimum of twice per week.
Relationships • Business associates	5%	No change required.
Relationships • Friends	2.5%	Email and call more frequently. One call and/or email every two weeks is sufficient. This doesn't take much of an effort.

Below is another snapshot of the same table as above, but with resources re-allocated after changing my lifestyle to be more balanced. I've been monitoring it closely and this seems to work best for me. Yours will look much different.

Priority	Percentage	Further Improvement Needed?
Career	60%	Workload too heavy to reduce further.
Health • Meal management	2.5%	No further change.
Health • Exercise	10%	No further change.
Health • Managing sleep optimally	2.5%	No further change.
Relationships • God	5%	No further change.
Relationships • Spouse/Significant Other	10%	Will monitor closely.
Relationships • Children	5%	No further change.
Relationships • Business associates	2.5%	No further change.
Relationships • Friends	2.5%	No further change.

There will be fewer negative surprises this way. Life is much better when you're proactively managing it.

Overview (So Far)

Up to this point, you've learned about the characteristics of a workaholic. You've also been schooled about the differences between a hard worker and a workaholic and how people become workaholics. The purpose for this section is to help you understand which of your strengths can be leveraged to help introduce balance into your life. Workaholics have many exemplary strengths. Those strengths should also be used to focus on improving your health and key relationships.

This section also highlights a workaholic's weaknesses. Some characteristics are worse than others and will be addressed in the next section. It's crucial for you to look at your life objectively before proceeding. Know where you stand and which strengths can be leveraged to improve your overall quality of life.

CHAPTER SIX

Prescriptions

Asking a workaholic to stop working crazy hours is futile. If they are highly productive and successful, why would they listen to anyone who tells them to slow down and relax? There is just no way they are going to allow for their momentum to get interrupted. I certainly didn't listen. That's not the solution, especially if you are not able to entice them with a better option. Even if you did manage to get their attention, then what? Would you rather have them become a couch potato like so many others or perhaps lounge around in bed every morning wasting precious time because they're no longer waking up with a purpose?

The trick here is not to *totally* stop everything you've been doing, just to smell the roses—not just yet anyway. Relaxing and enjoying the beauty around you is important, but a comprehensive plan (which includes fun time) to get you from where you are today to living a more balanced life is even more crucial. It's been clearly established that you're disciplined when it comes to work. *There's no reason you can't apply those same skill sets that made you successful into other areas of your life.*

Let's take a closer objective look at the solutions to the bad and ugly symptoms I highlighted in the beginning of this book. This isn't rocket science. They are very straightforward and doable, based on real-world experience—my life.

Introduce *Small* Simple Changes First

As you move forward toward building a better life, make small and calculated improvements in your daily living. Take baby steps to initiate change. Gradually introduce new non work-related activities into your daily routine. I'm referring to activities that will yield a good non-materialistic ROI.

Earlier in the book, I facilitated an evaluation for my colleague and friend Leticia. If you recall, she had quite a few weaknesses. After reviewing with me, she wasn't surprised at all. She took it well. Most people know their faults, but once they see it documented in one table—it's truly eye-opening and at times scary to see how much work is ahead. I also documented my strengths and weaknesses— no surprises there.

At first, you may not like what you see, but most people I evaluate like to know where they actually stand and the effort involved to correct the problems. As a full-time life coach, I facilitate hundreds of evaluations each year. The first step is to thoroughly understand a client's strengths and weaknesses. Don't try to conquer them all overnight. It's not going to happen. You simply don't have the resources to pull off this kind of miraculous transformation in a hurry. It's important to make small changes, one by one. This is also applicable when setting goals and establishing daily milestones. Typically people who set large goals fail miserably. Get used to small successes instead of living in a world of continuous failure. The key is to *consistently move forward.*

After I lost everything, I went back to the basics. It started with bringing spirituality back into my life. When I started to focus on relationships—making it a priority, I made a few more small changes. I would start by calling my mother every day. Prior to my big fall, I would rarely call. As usual, work got in the way. Once again, how pathetic of an excuse is that—not taking the time to call your own mother.

Because I was always consumed with work, she would end up calling me at least once a week. Unfortunately if we did connect,

I would rush her off the phone. On the occasions that we didn't connect, sometimes it would take me several weeks to call her back. I didn't even talk to her for two weeks at a time. Mind you, she was 80 years old and a cancer survivor. How do you think I would have felt if my mom had died and I had never called her because all I cared about was my next project? Making small changes in your life like calling your parents will groom you into being a better person, not to mention make you feel pretty darn good every day.

Solutions to the Bad and Ugly Characteristics

Below are the solutions to the bad and ugly characteristics I highlighted above. I separated the solutions into the three most critical priorities.

Career

It has to be a priority. You spend at least one-third of your life working, and even so most people just barely scrape by. For the workaholic (like myself) more than half of my life has been engulfed in working. A workaholic wants to make lots of money, possess power, and be successful. They have enormous egos that have to be fed continually. The competition is fierce out there in the workforce and to make the big bucks you need to really go that extra mile. Whatever resources you can muster need to be used to climb that corporate ladder. You have to prove your worth. You need to be noticed by upper management.

As you expend your energy day and night to make a mark in your professional world, there's typically very little left over for the other important areas in your life. This is the normal MO for the workaholic. Everything takes a back seat to your job. The bills don't let up and the cost of living keeps rising. These are the facts of life. Before you know it, your career sucks you in and eventually it will spit you out—like it did me. Be proactive and avoid some of the issues that have the potential to destroy your life. Heed the solutions below.

Mentor Key Staff to become High Performers

Problem: Micromanaging and controlling.

As a workaholic you have the tendency to be controlling and micromanage, because any mistakes coming out of your department is a bad reflection on you. Having the right team is imperative for you to live the balanced life that you seek. Putting together a winning team can really make the difference between success and failure in your career.

Be prepared because the possibilities will be endless. As much as you'll want to, don't micromanage. I know that's easier said than adhered to by a workaholic. But if you continue to hoard all the work, failure will be imminent. There will always be more work than resources in most successful companies, as well as startups. The hours you continue to invest will eventually take a toll on you. That, my friends, is a guarantee.

A number of studies have shown that executives who work 60 to 80-hour work weeks are less productive than the ones who put in 40 to 60 hours of work. Don't lie to yourself: you will need help from a strong and formidable team to be successful. Use your resources effectively by *mentoring key staff* to be better performers and some may even develop into viable leaders. You will always find a few who have the initiative and intelligence to excel in the organization.

If you're in management, it's important to have as many superstars as possible on your team. The better the performers, the easier it will be for you to adjust and manage your resources effectively to change your lifestyle. If you don't have a few good right-hand people as dependable as the sun, then you will need to start recruiting or begin mentoring some of your existing employees to become potential leaders and superstars.

You can start off by evaluating each of your key employee's strengths and weaknesses. This is the first step to building the right team. The ones who have potential are the ones you or a consultant should develop into superstars.

Evaluate Key Skills

Having a good team in place is easier said than done. Recruiting or developing a quality team requires resources like time and energy. Some resources you may not necessarily have. If you don't happen to have the bandwidth, hire an external consultant to come in and evaluate your team. Start by evaluating everyone's strengths and weaknesses. Look closely at their self-discipline, EQ, and leadership skills. These are the areas that are the most

critical for your employees to be proficient in:
- Self-discipline. They should be focused, self-motivated, possess a sense of urgency, efficient with time, goal-oriented, unwilling to procrastinate, structured, and with effective priorities.
- EQ (Emotional Quotient). They should be able to communicate effectively, have excellent inter-personal skills and manage relationships effectively.
- Leadership. Others should follow and produce.

Once you determine whether or not you have a few potential superstars then help those few sharpen their skills. Find out quickly who possesses the initiative to excel in their career. Identify those few and mentor them to take on more responsibility. It would be nice to have many superstars, but realistically, that is not likely to be the case. Out of a pool of ten good employees, you may only find two who could be mentored to excel.

High Performers

Take the time to mentor as many subordinates as possible to become high performers and leaders. They need to possess many of your skills—as if they were walking in your shoes. The more capable subordinates you employ or develop, the easier it will be to re-distribute your limited resources into your other priorities. Everyone wants to delegate more; however, recruiting and/or mentoring resourceful, skilled and dependable underlings is an exhaustive endeavor. Who has the time? If you want to get out of the rut you're in there has to be some sort of sacrifice. You have to invest the time. Unfortunately, there is no easy answer.

Good employees need and seek guidance. They hunger for mentors. It's a win-win situation. The process will actually allow you to not only improve employee performance, but it will also allow you to weed out dead weight. You'll know quickly enough who's worth the effort and who simply is not.

Story: Loser Turned High Performer

I needed a strong team to help me be successful. The more Harris Kern clones I had under my wing, the sooner I would be able to live a more balanced life. Matthew reported into my organization.

He was articulate, personable, charming, and intelligent. But he was a total loser, at least in my book. He was in his early thirties, in an entry-level position, a single father of one, and strictly a 9-to-5 kind of guy. He had the potential to be a superstar, but he was just squandering his life, going nowhere in his career.

Curiosity got the best of me and I decided to find out more about Matthew. I facilitated an evaluation to understand his strengths and weaknesses—also to know his career objectives. My assessment showed he was in horrible shape. He had gone through a divorce the year before. His wife had fallen in love with another man and had taken their only son to live in a different state. His career was going nowhere; he had been given a written warning for poor performance at work. He was on the verge of losing his job. Did I mention that he was also excessively thin due to eating no more than one meal a day? Yet, no one could really blame him; as a matter of fact, pretty much everyone felt sorry for him. His only outlet that helped him get through this harrowing chapter of his life was partying at the local bars several times a week. Because of his good looks and great personality, he had no problems meeting women.

Matthew and I became good friends. He would always help people—he was a genuinely nice guy although he was about to be booted out of the company. His boss was named Nancy. Nancy reported into me so I knew all about Matthew's terrible work performance. What I liked most about him was his personality, honesty, sincerity, loyalty and passion to succeed. People naturally gravitated towards him.

One weekday afternoon close to the end of the workday, I was walking into the Data Center to speak with a colleague. I looked over, and there was Matthew on the telephone with a big smile on his face. You could tell he was talking to some chick. Probably one he had just met. As a matter of fact there were always girls calling for Matthew. The scuttlebutt around the room was that anytime the phone rang, his fellow employees would say, "Oh, it's for you, Matthew." This was not the way one should be recognized at work. The perception others had of him was anything but favorable. He had actually become the joke of the entire organization.

As I walked over toward him, something inside of me went off like an explosion. By this time we were pretty good friends. I asked him whom he was talking to, and he uttered some girl's name. I did not care what her name was. I told him to hang up. He could see that I was not kidding around. I had a very stern look on my face, and he could tell something was up. Within five seconds, he hung up the phone. He asked me what the matter was.

"What time do you get off?" I asked Matthew.

He replied 5:00 P.M.

I asked him to come see me in my office right after his shift ended. He said he had some personal things to take care of. I told him those things could wait; he was probably meeting some girl for a drink after work anyway. He said okay.

Matthew came into my office at 5:05 P.M. He asked, "What's up?"

I replied, "Sit down, please." Now remember, Matthew did not report directly to me, he was two levels down, but I felt like he had potential to be a superstar, but required some serious coaching. For the next hour, I tore into him. There were moments when he actually broke down and cried.

"What are you doing with your life? Why are you throwing it all down the toilet? You are always complaining that you are overlooked for promotions, yet the perception in the Data Center is that you put forth no effort to receive one. Do you think that someone will come and hand you that promotion on a silver platter?" My tone was stern throughout the conversation. "Do you like working at this company?"

"Yes."

"But you've been in the same entry-level position for the past three years now." Right about then I felt like kicking him in the rear end and said, "I cannot believe you have been a Computer Operator for the past three years. Matthew, let me tell you where you are. Go buy a gun and point it at your head and fire, because you might as well be dead. You are a damn loser and failure."

This is not a generally recommended tactic, but I knew Matthew and how he'd respond. He was shocked, but he did not argue. I told him that he was going nowhere quickly. He agreed with me.

I said to him, "From this day forward things are going to change! This is your last opportunity to turn your career around." I knew he was listening. "Things WILL change. I am tired of listening to you whine about your current position and status. You

NEED to help yourself!"

At this point Matthew was very distraught. He asked what he needed to do.

I said, "Work is now the priority—your only priority!"

I was extremely rough on Matthew, never letting up on him, not even for a moment. I will never forget when he actually broke down and cried. It hurt me as well, but it had to be this way.

"Effective immediately," I said, "You will have a contract with yourself. You will adhere to the following rules and guidelines...

1. *You will not accept any non-urgent personal phone calls during working hours. The only phone calls you can accept will be from family members, yet those will be limited to one a day. You will tell them (in a nice way, of course) no more phone calls unless it is an urgent matter that needs to be addressed immediately.*

2. *You will put in extra hours every day. Ask your supervisor for special projects. Starting with tomorrow, you will no longer leave work at exactly 5:00 P.M. There will be no more clock-watching. You will put in an extra one or two hours each day to start with.*

At that point he looked at me and said, "But I won't get paid for those extra hours."

I said, "Yup! Think of it as donating your body to charity. You are going to make some wholesale sacrifices in your life. In other words, instead of spending 80% of your time on partying, you will spend 90% of your time rebuilding your career...

3. *We will sit down together and determine your next career move. Then you will have a discussion with your supervisor and manager to advise them that, from this day forward, your life and career is going to change. Based on your past performance, your management will probably not take you seriously, but that is okay. They know, just as I know, that anyone can talk—the hard part is performing. In addition, just as important to sustain that performance year after year.*

4. *Start training and studying for that next position. You might need to take some night courses, purchase books, or train with senior staff. Whatever the requirements for that*

next position are—you will gladly meet them!

5. *There will be no more dating until you achieve your goal.* (I knew this one would kill him because he was such a ladies' man.) *You will be working on projects and studying for that next position. No excuses whatsoever. You will not have a personal life until we turn this around.*

6. *You will provide me a weekly status report on your progress. That report will be due in to me every Monday morning by 8:00 A.M. sharp!*

Matthew replied, "But, Harris, my work shift doesn't begin until 9:00 A.M."

"Very good, my little buddy, you're starting to get the hang of how this works. Failure to comply with any of the above at any time means I am through mentoring you. You can continue to be a loser. I will still be your friend, but I will not waste my time. There are no guarantees this will work. Let's see if we can turn that perception that people have of you around with some constructive results."

The goal for Matthew was to get his act together and become a productive employee. A promotion would signify success.

"Oh yes, one more VERY important piece to this puzzle: you need to WANT to do this. I cannot force you to do this."

Matthew thought about it for about a moment, suddenly it became very quiet in my office.

"I really want to do this," he said emphatically.

"Are you sure?" I asked again. "This will be the most difficult and stressful ordeal you could possibly go through, next to your divorce. You will hate me at times. I take that back, you will probably hate me all the time, UNTIL the day you receive your promotion."

I told him that this would be a dramatic change in his lifestyle. It would be difficult for him or anyone else, for that matter to go through this ordeal.

"Now tell me, but before you respond, sit in here for thirty minutes and think about it." I started to leave my office. By this time it was 6:15 P.M. He was alone.

"Oh, by the way," I said as I was walking out, "I will not be angry if you say 'No'. This will not affect our friendship one way or another."

It was important for him to know that, and more importantly

to have an out. I did not want to force anyone into doing something they did not want to. I just knew that Matthew needed help and a big push; there was no way he could do it on his own.

When I returned, Mathew was sitting there quietly.

"Okay, bud, what will it be?"

"Yes," he replied.

"Are you sure?"

"YES!"

"Matthew, I am asking you one more time. It is okay to say no. I will still value our friendship, BUT if you quit half way through this ordeal, I will be very disgusted with you."

Over the next year and a half, Matthew changed in a big way. Not only did he abide by the guidelines I set for him, but he also attended night school to acquire some applicable skills. To top that off, he never went out on a single date during the entire period. Don't worry, he started dating again, but only when he was ready. He had become a very different person. He was beaming with confidence.

By the way, I almost forgot to mention... Matthew was promoted out of the data center! Then, a pleasant surprise: he was promoted again, twice within three years.

Establish and Nurture Key Relationships—Stop Hoarding

Problem: Controlling all projects.

Communicate regularly with individuals who can help you be successful (colleagues, peers, consultants, and management). Schmooze with them to advance *your* own agenda. Individuals who you can depend on to deliver your projects on schedule and on budget are the ones you should have on your radar. First, find out who they are. Do your homework—ask lots of questions— indiscriminately of course. Do not waste precious and limited cycles fraternizing with the wrong, toxic people. The only way to allot more time for your personal life is to bond with people who can meet that objective.

Take the time to *continuously* communicate with the *right* individuals (i.e., perhaps take short breaks together or even go out to lunch regularly). You can't do it all yourself. In time, refusal to delegate will give way to a desire to work practically and an appreciation for working collectively.

Learn to be a Nice Asshole

Now that you've included health and relationships into your life as priorities, time will be even more precious and scarce than ever before. In general, people love to babble. It's the number one time-waster at the office. It's everywhere you go: in meetings, in the break room, people stopping by your office, in the restroom, in the hallway, etc. Learn to cut them off—respectfully, without hurting their feelings. *Learn to say no with grace.*

Some of these methods may not seem appropriate, but utilizing scarce resources to their fullest sometimes requires unusual measures. I referred to myself as a *nice asshole*. That label is still associated with me today. Everywhere I go, people just love to babble. You really have no choice, if you want to be successful living a more balanced lifestyle you need to manage your scarce resources effectively.

Minutes are precious! As an executive and owner of multiple businesses I was constantly bombarded by what I refer to as *discussions of nonsense* or *content-free speech*. Here are some techniques that will help you effectively manage the many distractions that life is capable of throwing your way. Learn to:

- Politely excuse yourself from any situation you feel is a waste of time or not associated with your priorities. It might be fun, but is it vital?
- Manage excruciatingly painful detail-oriented people effectively. Normally, these are the individuals who have to spell out every letter of every word and take forever to get to the point. Speed up an individual's slow conversation without being rude or offensive. Remember to really acknowledge them so they feel heard and don't need to repeat themselves.

In this era of having to do more with less resources, being a nice asshole is a necessary evil. People are the biggest time wasters. You don't want to hurt someone's feelings so say no in the right manner. There's no way to be successful without managing your time efficiently.

Story: The Nice Guy

Dennis was a friend of mine. Unfortunately we've lost touch with each other over the past decade. He was a brilliant man with a great personality. Professionally, he was a senior IT executive and an author. We worked together at Sun Microsystems, where he supported sales and marketing by speaking to customers about how to implement and manage complex computing systems. Subject matter experts like Dennis were always in demand by our sales organization.

Dennis had a major weakness that prevented him from effectively managing his other priority—his health. He had several health related goals—to lose weight and exercise consistently. However, he could never get to either one. Dennis spread himself thin all over the place—trying to help his co-workers. Dozens of sales representatives throughout his geographic territory, each with up to a dozen customers, all wanted him to meet with their customers. When he co-authored his first book (with me), *Building the New Enterprise*, the demand for his services had gone global.

As a result, work had consumed his life, with no end in sight. He usually worked 12 to 14 hours a day, and by the time he got home, he was too wiped out to do anything for himself. He realized that the only way to achieve his health related goals was to put an honest effort into reprioritizing his life. And it had to start by saying no at work, so that he could get his hours back down to around 10 a day. The nice thing for him was that he had control over his schedule. It wasn't a requirement to work that many hours.

There were several effective ways Dennis could have said no without ruining his "nice guy" reputation or offending someone. Here are just two examples:

- "Management has asked me to work on some very critical projects. I'd love to meet with your customer, but can it please wait until next month?"
- "I truly would love to help you out, but can I please get back to you as soon as I can, maybe in the next two weeks? My travel schedule has been overwhelming and I really need to spend some time with my family. I hope you don't mind."

There are also many ways NOT to say no:
- "I'm busy."

- "I have more important things to do."
- "I will get to it when I have the time."

Of course, the worst thing of all is to say yes and then not do it! If you are known as a hard worker with integrity, then people will generally understand if you tell them that you are too busy in a nice way. However, committing to something and then not following through is the surest way to wreck your integrity and reputation.

The same principles apply to your home life and to the always-difficult balance between home and work. Sometimes you will have to say no to your spouse and kids, and for many, that's even harder than saying no to a coworker or even your boss.

The bottom line: sear your priorities and goals into your brain. Use them as guidelines to determine what you can commit to, and what is too much. Then learn to say no.

Perception and Management's Radar 24x7

Problem: Worried about not being on management's radar 24x7 for career advancement.

It's important to demonstrate that you're a company person day and night. This means investing extra hours in the evenings and on the weekends. Be prepared to put in an ungodly amount of hours if necessary. Sometimes it will be unavoidable. But other times you may be able to outsmart management by making it appear that you're working more hours than you actually are.

Let's say you typically work 60-hour weeks. If you follow these simple steps, it will appear to management that you're working 80-hour weeks. This is what I call the WOW factor. In the corporate world it's all about perception. You shouldn't think of it as lying. Consider it more like battlefield tactics to outmaneuver or outsmart your enemy. Do it in a method where it looks like you're investing more hours than you actually are.

Let's say it's Wednesday and your project completion date is the following Monday. Do as much as possible Monday through Friday and even if you finish your project Friday afternoon, don't email the deliverable just yet—wait until the weekend. It's all about winning that perception battle, the biggest one in the corporate world. Every manager looks at the time stamp on emails that come in during off-hours. Work-related emails you send during these off hours will draw management's attention. They will typically recognize you as a company person. They believe you're thinking about your job day and night. You're doing whatever it takes to get the job done.

Following this simple piece of advice will make it appear as though you're working around the clock on your projects. Do your best to resist the urge to email the deliverable upon completion. Instead hold on to it and then send the deliverable Saturday evening or Sunday morning. You are still submitting your deliverable ahead of schedule, but it appears in the eyes of management that you've worked throughout the weekend. Congratulations, you've just won a strategic battle. It's also a good idea to work an extra few hours to catch up in a quiet environment. An early Saturday morning before your family wakes up is ideal. Send email to management and your staff throughout the weekend. Once again, the perception is you've been working around the clock. But in reality, you're not, and that goes a long way.

Other things you can do to make a good impression and get ahead is outmaneuver management and fight back in the politically correct manner. *Play the corporate game* and do it well, especially when interacting with management during the week about a certain project that has been assigned to you with some unrealistic demands attached to it. As much as you may want to, don't say no—tell them you'll work on it over the weekend and send the deliverable before Monday. For example, make sure they remember (be subtle) that your current customer-related responsibilities will fill up the work week and you didn't want to drop the ball on anything. Don't make it look like you're complaining. It's just a gentle reminder that your plate is full and you'll get to this very important project over the weekend when it's easier to complete the work without interruption. Make sure you work on it during the week, but don't tell your boss that. Complete as much as possible before the weekend, but hit send over the weekend—preferably on Sunday. It's critical you be subtle about it, make sure they know over casual conversations that you worked over the entire weekend.

The same advice goes for status emails. Complete them and place each one in your Draft Email folder—then click *Send* in the evening. It looks like you're working around the clock, but you're actually not. If you want to be noticed think and strategize constantly, don't just do. One more thing, don't communicate directly with management. Do it indirectly. For instance, if someone asks how your weekend was, consider responding this way, "It was excellent. I had fun with the family and accomplished a great deal on my big project."

Think Strategic

Problem: Missing out on that promotion.

If you want to improve your odds of getting that promotion, don't wait for your boss to bark out orders. Don't wait for management to assign you tasks. Be proactive. Look around to see what needs fixing or which functions could be performed in a much more expedient and efficient manner. Perhaps design a new process to streamline the way the marketing department interacts with the sales department. There's always room for improvement in every organization. The trick here is to not work with blinders on. Constantly assess the environment to see if you can make suggestions to eliminate unnecessary bureaucracy.

Gradually Cut Back

Problem: Working extraordinary long hours.

It's important to recharge your batteries. When you work too many hours you're thinking, creativity, productivity, communication, and cooperation is non-existent. Never mind the damage it's doing to your health. So you're working around the clock. You love it—it doesn't faze you a bit. You're actually turned on by it. But it's unhealthy for you in every aspect of your existence (physical, emotional, spiritual and personal). It's time to wise up and cut back in a very structured and calculated manner. You need to start with weekends. Manage those numbers first.

If you are consistently working ten hours every weekend, gradually cut back until you're only investing six to eight hours of time over the entire weekend. Perhaps work a few hours each morning or all on Saturday and take Sunday off. The era of turning your work completely off every weekend is long gone. Doing more with less for the company is here to stay, unfortunately, but *taking small steps to invest in other areas of your life can go a long way to living a happier, healthier, satisfying, and, yes, even a more productive life.* The more you re-charge your batteries, the more productive you will become.

Prioritize or You Will Fail

Problem: Taking on too much all at once.

There's no way you are going to do everything you want to do as quickly as you want. That's what makes life so challenging: there's always more to do. The problem is your resources are limited. I've accomplished dozens of major goals and hundreds of minor ones, but even in my elder years, I've got plenty more to accomplish, with new goals popping up all the time. Without accomplishments you're merely existing—live by accomplishing more. Workaholics like myself are addicted to accomplishments. I don't want that to EVER change. For me, living life is all about accomplishments, in every facet of it.

Make sure that all of your tasks and obligations fall within the three major priorities. If they do not, place them elsewhere for now. Once you identify everything and the amount of time each task or obligation takes, determine which ones are truly necessary. Under-schedule and allow more time than you think you need for each task, allowing enough time to be able to accept the unexpected. It's important to establish and maintain this type of structure to have a better quality of life. Document everything you need to accomplish for any given day on your to-do list then prioritize those activities. Follow and maintain your list judiciously. Make sure you establish that list every evening to use that next day.

Money is Important but NOT Everything

Problem: Never enough money and toys syndrome.

I have money and toys—so what? I had even more toys when I was in my thirties and forties. At the age of 60, I own several homes, including a condo on the beach in Florida with a million-dollar view, but none of that excites me and it doesn't fulfill my life. Sure, it's nice to have. We all need additional income and a place to have some fun. But it doesn't make me genuinely happy. It's just an investment for my family. When I see them happy, that warms my heart. I've learned the hard way that money-hunger is a superficial and hollow mentality. Money is tangible, but it ends there. It certainly is one way to measure success, but it's the least important in the grand scheme of things.

Tell me, what good are all these material things without my family? Nothing. There's nothing more valuable than that. I know so because all I had at one time were my toys and money. At my age, these two things do not keep me from feeling empty and alone. The undeniable truth is you're going to leave this planet just the way you came in, with *nothing*. And there is a rather simple solution. Open your eyes, kill that ego, and please listen to me—invest time (your most valuable resource) into your family while you have them at your side, otherwise you may just lose them like I did.

Work from Home When You're Sick

Problem: Going into the office when you're sick and contagious.

I can't condone your actions. It's what I always did—work through illness. Prior to the Internet, a workaholic rarely missed a day of work due to being sick. He or she went into the office regardless of how contagious they were or how badly they felt. They didn't care if they contaminated others. Times are different now. In the networked world we live in today, workaholics don't have to go into the office when they're sick. Yet some still want to maintain their impeccable attendance record and so they show up to work when they should clearly be at home recuperating. Do everyone a big favor and stay home—get ample rest. You can still do your work from home in-between resting and sleeping and you won't contaminate others.

Recharging Your Batteries

Problem: Not getting enough rest and relaxation.

What made it more difficult for me was how I trained my mind by playing mind games (explained further in my book titled *Going from Undisciplined to Self-Mastery*) to push myself harder to work longer hours and be more productive. *Deliver, deliver and deliver more!* was my battle cry. My internal struggles to accomplish more never eased up. I learned how to recharge my batteries as quickly as possible to be more creative, resourceful, and productive.

When friends or family used to tell me to relax and take it easy, I would usually respond by saying that relaxation was meant for humans who are always whining about being tired. I then made the case that a well-oiled machine like me didn't need to relax very often. Furthermore, I would tell them that I would relax plenty in death. The excitement of tackling yet another accomplishment kept me vibrant and full of energy. It kept my adrenalin flowing day and night. I rarely broke down and if I did, no one would know.

Relaxation was a four-letter word for me. Now I realize that was a masochistic and stupid mentality to have. We all need to relax and get ample rest to remain energetic and healthy. That line of reasoning back then was stupid and it still is. We all know we have to recharge.

However, that doesn't mean shutting everything off. For me it meant that when I was tired, I'd take a shower and perhaps watch something that I liked on TV for thirty minutes or even sit through an entire movie with my family.

I know perfectly well it's hard to tear yourself away from work. You aren't likely to listen to experts who tell you to slow down or relax. But it is in your best interest to listen to reason. When you do relax, your mind is recharged, and as a result, you'll become much more productive.

When I introduced more balance into my life on my own terms it actually included different ways to relax in order to make me more productive. When I put "the R-word" in terms of productivity, then, and only then, I could relate.

Do simple things throughout the day to help you re-charge. If you have an office with a door, close it, put your feet up on the desk, and learn how to take a twenty minute power nap. Trust me: it is going to feel great. If you're an early riser and you've already exercised that morning, take that power nap mid-morning or mid-afternoon. Another method of relaxation is to take a walk around your building if the weather permits. It's a great way to blow off some stream and get some fresh air. You might try going out to lunch once a week with a colleague. I say once a week because you don't want to pick up any counterproductive habits like going out to lunch too frequently.

On the weekend you should also schedule some sort of physical activity. This could be walking, swimming, playing basketball, washing the car, cleaning the house, or even working in the garden on a nice summer day. The idea is to do something outdoors, especially if the weather is cooperative. It might take some experimenting to find an activity you enjoy, so feel free to try out different things.

Another thing you can do is schedule some quiet time. Whether it's meditation each morning, stretching, or reading something non-work related for fifteen minutes, you should do it in silence, alone with no distractions. Once you're consistent with your new routine, you may want to increase the time you've allocated toward relaxation.

Among non-workaholics, who doesn't love to relax or just be totally lazy and do nothing for an entire day? It's actually healthy for you and will contribute to your overall happiness. For the disciplined workaholic like myself, that is impossible to do—don't go there. You will stress yourself out even further. Proactively relaxing a few minutes a day is a good thing. Total relaxation is extremely difficult. It's a totally different mindset. Now that's the understatement of the year. You need to start looking at it as just another task to help you excel in your other two priorities of health and relationships. If you improve upon your health and relationships, you will definitely continue to excel in your career. Instilling some sort of relaxation techniques into your routine could also save your marriage in the long run—trust me on that one.

Your body and mind needs an outlet—it also has to recuperate. If you don't maintain a healthier lifestyle and recharge your mind and body, something will eventually go wrong. So-called experts say you will burn out. Quite frankly, I don't believe that. Workaholics don't burn out, but they destroy other areas of their life. *Burnout* is not in their vocabulary. However, it is a necessity to proactively find methods of relaxation ASAP.

Story: The Perfect Solution for Vacations and Workaholics

I'm going to make this story short and to the point. Whether we accept it or not, we all need vacations. Spending quality time with family or someone special is an essential human need that simply can't be ignored. There's no argument there. Throughout my life, I have slept very little in comparison to my wife and children. They easily slept twice as much as I did. On one occasion, my wife, the children and I were in Puerto Rico on vacation. I would get up after my minimal sleep, go to the hotel gym, manage my email, take a shower and be back in bed before anyone woke up. It's easier to do a little bit every day then it is to have more than a thousand emails waiting for you when you get back. How stressful is that? There goes your rest and relaxation. However, since I managed mine while on vacation, I wasn't stressed when I returned to the office. I even found time to enjoy the pool and beach and have fun with my family when I was on vacation.

Be Proactive in Your Personal Life

Problem: Avoiding emotional issues by drowning yourself with more work.

We all know that being proactive in your personal life and dealing with issues consume a humungous amount of resources. They can stop your productivity dead in its tracks—in a heartbeat. In your new balanced world, where you're focusing on your relationships and health, be proactive and communicate regularly with your significant other.

I know everyone is always busy, but it will save a lot of grief in the long run. What's thirty to sixty minutes a day? Don't ignore personal issues—like yours truly used to do. Even if you think they are trivial, your spouse may think differently. Make sure to include discussions with your significant other in your daily routine. Turn the TV off and talk while you're cooking dinner or gathered around the dinner table. Be sure to include discussions in your nightly routine and also document movie time, pet projects, and similar items on your to-do list.

Health

Your mind needs your body in perfect condition. By perfect I mean the best condition that you're able to achieve given your circumstances. Without your body in the best mint condition you will be adding another obstacle on your road to success. Your body and mind need to work in harmony as one.

Exercise Every Single Day

What exactly is exercise? The dictionary defines exercise as intentional motion for the purpose of being fit. The idea is to move and to do it often. Any movement is better than no movement at all. If you find yourself avoiding exercise, think of times that you enjoyed moving your body? Was it playing sports, exploring, dancing, walking? If you associate exercise with pleasure then you will feel more motivated to do it.

Let's see how many ways you can think of to make exercising fun for you. Ask your friends to join you in a brainstorming session.

Does belly dancing do it for you? Is getting out with the guys playing basketball more your thing? Do you stay on the treadmill longer if you're listening to your favorite music? Once you pinpoint what fun is for you then you'll exercise and continue doing it on a regular basis.

Here are some guidelines to follow:

- *Be consistent.* Consistency is the key to success with any milestone. Do whatever it takes to complete your exercise milestone every day. Whether you're cleaning your apartment one day, walking around the block the next, going to the gym yet another day—do it daily—it will eventually become habitual. Your mind needs to get used to accomplishments versus failures every day.
- *Establish doable targets.* If you're someone who has difficulties achieving exercise-related goals, be realistic and start small, with attainable milestones. Exercise twice a week to begin with or even once a week. When you're consistently achieving your initial milestones, increase your frequency, perhaps to two or three times a week.
- *Maintain a Personal Banking System (PBS).* The concept is simple. It's the same notion as putting money away in a savings account in case it's needed for an emergency. Except this isn't about finances, it's about investing in a healthy lifestyle. Let's say your milestone is to exercise twice a week. The objective is to always try to do more. If you exercise more than two times on any given week, deposit the extra workouts into your PBS and build a nest egg. Emergencies will occur and if you don't have a savings of workouts to withdraw from then you will have a setback.

The goal is to never withdraw from your PBS. Unfortunately, in life, emergencies do happen, so be prepared, stay ahead of the game and remain healthy. The reward will be your increased ability to control your body, have fun with it, and a reserve of physical endurance, which comes in handy when the baby keeps you up all night.

- *Make exercise fun.* Exercise doesn't have to be unpleasant, yet so many people look upon it as a necessary evil with nothing but sweat and unnecessary pain. There are many other things that people would rather be doing. So get creative. How can you make it fun? Do you like variety? Would you prefer to work out with a partner? Are you the kind of person who always needs support from someone else? Do you need incentives? Is dancing something you like to do? Are you the outdoor type who likes to commune with nature? Is it more fun when it's a group? Do you like to compete against yourself or others?

- *Define exercise criteria.* Our bodies need some form of exercise on a regular basis, but you don't have to go to the gym each day. Walk up and down the stairs instead of always using the elevator. Choose a day and clean your house vigorously or wash and wax the car. Lifting weights, running, or long brisk walks are also creative ways to exercise. Train your mind that cleaning the house is exercise, as is washing and waxing the car. It really works. You'll get a pretty good sweat out of it and accomplish two things at once.

Promoting a Healthy Routine each Morning

After your morning devotionals and prayers, start every day with a health-conscious regimen. Living a healthy lifestyle is not up for debate. You have one life—improve your odds for longevity. Obviously you love what you do—why not do it for as long as you can? Begin each day with some sort of exercise routine. Get those endorphins going first thing in the morning. You'll feel good about yourself mentally, be much more energetic and get your day started off on the right track with your engine turning at a very high RPM. Is that too much to ask? You've just added some balance into your life in a big way. Now treat every day equally and do this seven days a week.

Be Consistent. Do it in the Morning

Problem: Not exercising consistently.

Exercise every morning before going to the office. Doing so will give those endorphins a strong jolt and make you feel twice as energetic for the rest of the day. We both know once you get to work it's difficult to get out at a reasonable hour to exercise. Besides, at the end of the day, you are usually too drained emotionally and physically, and the health clubs are jam packed between 5 to 9 P.M.

Most people will find it difficult to muster up the energy to exercise after a twelve-plus hour day. It's a legitimate excuse. There will always be excuses preventing you from working out in the evenings—probably every night. It's an awesome feeling to start each day with a major accomplishment, besides the fact that it's good for you!

I can't stress enough just how important it is to do some form of exercise daily. If you are unable to make it to the gym one morning, then take a quick walk around the block or around your office building at a brisk pace. If the weather is bad, try doing some sit-ups and pushups at home before leaving for the office. The key is doing some sort of activity daily. We all know the importance of maintaining good health and that exercise is a necessity, and it will provide you with more energy to be more productive at work first thing in the morning.

Without good health, you have nothing—we all know this. Most workaholics use the same lame excuse, "I don't have time to exercise." Hogwash! Everyone has 30 to 60 minutes a day to do something good for themselves. But okay, I'll play along. Let's say you really don't have the time. What's the harm of working 11.5 hours and spending 30 minutes on exercise? Absolutely none!

Establish a new daily work routine that encompasses exercise. Including exercise into your routine is easier said than done. Making exercise habitual on paper or in your mind is one thing, but consistently doing it is a whole different story altogether. Workaholics typically cancel anything not work-related due to unrealistic project/task deadlines or calls from the boss. We all know that work emergencies have a way of cropping up at the most inopportune time. That's why it's important to train your mind to believe that exercise is just an extension of your career.

To recap: treat every day equally by doing some form of exercise before going to work each morning. Don't bother doing it after work. We know how crowded the gyms are at this time of day. Besides you are likely to be too exhausted by the end of the day and you'll use this as the perfect excuse not to go. Train your mind to believe that exercise is part of your daily work routine. Tell yourself repeatedly that if you don't exercise all the effort put forth into your career will be for nothing because you'll probably die of a heart attack. Repeat this until you actually believe it. Sure it's hardcore negativity, but paint the ugliest scenario and your mind will eventually start believing it and force you to exercise daily.

Just like work is a daily occurrence for the workaholic, exercise must be part of your morning work routine. It's easier to train the mind to exercise every day than it is to exercise three days a week. Let's say you get up at 7 A.M. to be at work by 9 A.M. Just get out of bed thirty minutes earlier and get in some exercise. On the positive side you know that exercise gets the endorphins going each day and will give you much more energy than drinking several cups of coffee.

Please Stop the Nonsense Excuses

"I'm too exhausted to exercise" or "I'm too tired" have to be the most widely and frequently used excuses. I hear it everywhere I go. That is such crap and you know it. If you exercised first thing each morning, then there would be no reason to use these lame excuses. Include exercise each morning prior to stepping foot into the office. If you're exhausted, so what? You have to get up anyway—what's the big deal about taking a quick walk around the block? Exercising in the morning has so many benefits. The number one reason is THERE'S NO BETTER WAY TO START EACH DAY! Just do it! It also...

- *Ensures consistency.* One of the most important words when it comes to exercise is consistency. It really doesn't do any good if you do it every day for one week and then you miss the next three weeks. If you exercise in the morning (like me), chances are you will be more consistent than individuals who exercise in the evening. Exercising in the morning pretty much guarantees that it doesn't get bumped due to a hectic afternoon or evening schedule or already having worked ten hours. There is no way you will feel like exercising that evening.
- *Promotes quality sleep.* Since you have to wake up earlier, exercise conditions your body to go to sleep earlier. As you expend energy earlier and throughout the day you will be more tired and sleep sounder at night. Research has demonstrated that people who exercise on a regular basis

have a higher quality of sleep and thus require less.

- *Cleans the slate.* It helps clear the mind of any negativity first thing in the morning.
- *Makes you much more energetic.* It gets those endorphins going, which improve your energy levels. It also jumpstarts your metabolism and keeps it elevated for hours. You'll be energized throughout the day.
- *Is a GREAT feeling.* I look forward to it each morning. Not only does it get my juices flowing, but I know I am doing something good for my body.
- *Encourages healthier eating habits.* A regular exercise routine in the morning changes your attitude about food. A healthy mindset makes it easier to resist temptation from bad foods.
- *Wakes up the brain faster.* It sharpens the mind before taking on the heavy load of the day. It's been proven to help you create mental focus and acuity for up to eight hours a day.
- *Helps you manage weight effectively.* Mornings are the optimal exercise times to maintain a healthy weight. It's been shown to reduce those bad food cravings throughout the day. When you exercise first thing in the morning, your body will use stored energy in the form of fats. The more efficient your metabolism, the more energy the body requires therefore more fat is burned. Stored fat is one of the main culprits of weight gain. By exercising first thing in the morning you're raising your metabolism, your body will be in fat burning mode the rest of the day, therefore helping you maintain the ideal weight.
- *Has a great cardiovascular impact.* We all know the importance of a good cardiovascular workout—to improve your heart health—right? One of the ways your body naturally wakes up is by increasing levels of hormones like adrenaline, which causes your heart to beat faster.
- *Builds confidence:* Early A.M. workouts are a great confidence builder. Once you get through your workout, the better you feel mentally and physically, and the more positive and happier you are!

Exercise is not an option. It's truly a matter of life or death. Don't be a fool—if you're a machine (workaholic) like me, you need to be lubed daily to maintain efficiency. So what are you waiting for? EXERCISE!

Train Your Mind to Consistently Exercise

Train your mind by telling yourself repeatedly that if you don't start exercising you are going to die of a heart attack or be crippled by a severe stroke. Use negative phrases to train your mind. In other words, scare the crap out of yourself when you feel an excuse coming on. But to train your mind effectively you need to rehearse your lines like you mean them. If you don't like negativity, then train your mind to exercise consistently by using positive affirmations: *If I exercise before work, I will be twice as energetic (the juices will be flowing), therefore twice as productive.* I personally liked the negative ones. They're a rude awakening sometimes. But no two people are alike.

You set goals and you're constantly strategizing when it comes to your career. You even establish key milestones to ensure you're progressing according to plan. Why can't you do the same in your personal life? You can and you should. Think about it for a minute. What's the point of being so successful in your professional world if you get a heart attack because you never exercise, or if your spouse decides to leave you because you rarely give your relationship the attention it deserves?

Managing Your Eating Habits

In my opinion, the English language should abolish the word *diet*. I hate it with a passion. Unfortunately, there are so many books written with the word *diet* as the subject matter it has brainwashed much of the population. Eating smart has nothing to do with dieting—diets rarely work. It's all about managing your intake. You don't have to read a "diet" book to figure this stuff out.

What to Eat and When

To maintain a healthy weight, you may simply need to change your eating habits. It's all about strict maintenance of your carbohydrate intake as well as portion control. Eat the bulk of your carbohydrates in the morning and at lunch. If you feel the urge to eat some carbohydrates in the evening, only do it occasionally, for instance once a week, and keep the portions very small.

We know what you're thinking. Where do desserts fit into this plan? Once you've got your mind and body used to this way of eating you'll be able to indulge in sweets once in a while and preferably at lunch (since they are carbohydrates), but don't make a habit of it. The less you submit to them the better off you'll be. The longer the time between eating desserts the better; since you'll just crave them less if you don't indulge in them quite as often. Once a week if you must, but don't forget; the harder you are working on your daily workouts the less you will crave the things that are obstacles to achieving your physical goal. Eating properly is about having control.

Don't Diet, Manage Caloric Intake

Problem: Difficulty losing weight and then maintaining it.

Eating smart has nothing to do with dieting. Play mind games to train your brain to effectively manage your eating habits. Some examples of mind games could be:

- Get a photo of a body you would like to have and look at it every day.
- Tell yourself daily that your body is strong and healthy and that it chooses the right foods to keep it so.
- Practice stress techniques to reduce comfort eating.
- Team up with someone who needs to get healthy and help them out.
- Find a partner who encourages you.
- A person's ability to accomplish something is only limited by their own self-doubt. (Repeat this to yourself many times).
- Make an image board that represents the benefits of the body you are aiming for. It's all about strict maintenance of your carbohydrate intake (breads, pasta, potatoes and rice) as well as portion control (total number of calories consumed). It's all about learning to control the urges of your body.
- You do have the ability to say no. You can regain your power over food. You can stop being hypnotized by food and the demands of your fat cells. Try this exercise when you are not hungry: Take an item of food you tend to eat too much of and examine it. Notice everything about it. Become aware

of the feelings you get while doing this exercise. Notice how your body responds to this item. Imagine having so much of this item of food that you can afford to waste it. Pretend you have huge quantities of it then throw it away. Now play games with it. Make up funny rules such as *I can only eat it on Saturdays.* Imagine stuffing yourself with it till you're sick of it. Then get the idea of having a very small portion of it.

Now decide you're going to eat it now, then change your mind and decide you're going to eat it later. Do the above exercise with several items of food that you crave. Notice the changes that occur in your eating habits.

If you indulge one day, cut back the next. Become aware of your caloric intake. However, don't waste precious cycles by measuring calories every meal unless you have nothing better to do with your time. Since most workaholics skip out on exercise, they need to eat healthier (fruits, vegetables, protein, and complex carbohydrates).

Case Study

As a speaker, author, IT consultant, organization mentor and life coach, I meet with a variety of people with different backgrounds and professions every day. Some of these individuals eventually become clients. One very interesting lady was a personal trainer who had many goals, which included becoming a professional bodybuilder. She was in her mid-twenties and was obsessed with her exercise routine and nutrition. Although she had many other goals in life, she would spend an enormous amount of time planning her daily workout routine, exercise, meal planning and diet. She would easily spend 4 to 5 hours each day on nutrition and exercise. She worked out hard and was constantly refining her routine. When she was in her early twenties she actually competed professionally as a bodybuilder. Health and fitness were her life and consumed her day and night.

Her routine was extremely complicated. I had no clue as to why anyone would want to follow such a highly complex routine. I remember the first time I reviewed her workout regimen—it made my head spin. It must have taken at *least* one hour a day to think about it and write it down. Can you imagine taking that long to strategize and write down a routine every day? Not me.

I've been working out for the past four-plus decades so I know a thing or two of what bodybuilders go through. I actually used to work out with several professional bodybuilders when I was in my early twenties. Their entire life was about nutrition, supplements, exercise and, yes, even steroids. That's all they cared about. However, she wanted to excel in other areas of her life just as badly.

As one can imagine, she was in stellar condition but, her entire focus was on health—she was a total healthaholic. Her desire was to compete again... or at least that's what she thought she wanted to do. Although she spent a lot of time planning and obsessing about her workouts, nutrition and supplements, she wasn't making the progress she was expecting. She was also missing quite a few workouts. She wasn't very consistent, because she had planned workouts so elaborately that even she couldn't keep up with her own system. Eventually, she realized that there was more to life than just bodybuilding. She wanted to focus on her personal training business, be consistent, and simplify her workouts as well. That's when she came to me for help.

She was so addicted to her workouts and managing her diet that she never had the time to strategize and develop a roadmap on how to grow her business. She lacked structure, didn't follow a routine, and couldn't hold herself accountable. She was also inconsistent in many areas: not following through on her workouts and not prioritizing her life to achieve her goals. It was critical for her to start her workout every morning by 3:00 A.M. Her first client started training with her at 5 A.M., Monday through Friday. She lived in Pittsburgh (EST) and I lived in Dallas (CST). I would call her each morning to make sure she got going and was at the gym by 3:30 A.M. (EST). I needed to get her on track quickly. The workouts were the most effective way to get the adrenalin going each morning. Once one was completed, she felt great. But that's the case for everyone. The hard part is being consistent and getting started. There's nothing better than starting each morning with a good exercise routine.

She was still putting very little effort into her business. All she was doing was training clients. There was no strategy: no business planning, no marketing program, no roadmap for growth. Needless to say, she was frustrated because she was going nowhere quickly. After facilitating a thorough evaluation to understand her strengths, weaknesses and goals, we decided that although she loved bodybuilding, it was no longer the *only* priority in her life. I had to transform her to live a more balanced lifestyle. It wasn't only about her health. I needed to incorporate a focus on business and relationships into her life.

Changing the Mindset

It wasn't going to be easy to prescribe a cure, especially to someone as physically fit as she was. At first appearance, she could be featured on the front cover of any fitness magazine, wearing a bikini. She was in superb shape. The true challenge for me was going to be to change her way of thinking. She was the ultimate healthaholic, but she didn't see it that way and certainly didn't feel the need for major change, only minor tweaking (she thought) so she could be more consistent.

The disease was lodged in deeply. I had one shot at changing her mind. I needed to get buy-in on a new strategy, one that would introduce balance into her life without using the word "balance." Although I knew the solution, I couldn't force it down her throat. She had to find out in due time and in a very calculated manner. It meant introducing a roadmap that would depict successes in other areas of her life. The prescription had to be administered in small dosages or I was going to lose the battle and possibly the war.

I made a few recommendations and she agreed. I told her that her health regimen was way too complicated. If she wanted to be a professional bodybuilder for the next X number of years then it wasn't the time to grow her business. There just weren't enough hours in the day. I was being very direct as always. If she wanted to grow her business and spend some quality time with her boyfriend we had to make time for her other priorities. Something had to give. I put it all on the table. "If you want to grow your business you have to make the time." She decided to forego the goal of being a professional bodybuilder and grow her business instead. She had no choice. She needed to move out of her parents' home. In order to do that, she had to increase her income to buy a home.

The Cure

We established three priorities: *business, health and relationships.* All three were important and all deserved equal billing. However, she couldn't spend days and nights on health and neglect her business any longer. We reduced her workout to one hour a day. The extra hours were devoted to her business and to actually develop a relationship with her boyfriend who was always placed on the back-burner.

We developed a roadmap to grow her business. I had her establish a to-do list every night for the next day and documented a new routine, which included focusing on daily milestones. We also had her maintain structure. At first she wasn't very organized—now she is.

Gradually, she began to realize that there was more to life than spending 4 to 5 hours a day on her health routine. She needed to be consistent in all areas—with all of her goals. Once she agreed on the strategy and roadmap, it was time to begin. My job was to hold her accountable to her to-do list (action items) seven days a week. She was an excellent pupil. She quickly found out that there was more to life than just bodybuilding and the challenges with growing her business were quite stimulating—a major rush. She was now being consistent in the three major areas of life.

Relationships

After focusing so much effort on your career and maintaining a healthy lifestyle, how much time is truly left over for relationships? Not much—if any. This is reality and it happens to be the most challenging area to deal with, mostly because it's the most complex and there are so many mixed emotions involved. As if it wasn't complicated enough, there's another person involved in this equation that you can't control. The inability to keep another person in line, especially your significant other, can really drive a workaholic crazy. Most of us must always be in total control of our environment and everyone who steps into it. When it comes to your career it's pretty much up to you to climb the corporate ladder. When your health is at stake then it's just you against that person in the mirror. I had no problem with that. But where I fell completely apart was having additional cycles left over to manage a relationship.

Faith First

Problem: Abandoning your faith.

Once I made the decision to do it, reconnecting with God was easy to pull off. Even reciting daily prayers and devotions did not prove to be difficult at all. It's still me, myself and I dealing with my spirituality. Below are the solutions to those bad and ugly characteristics highlighted in the beginning of the book to do with relationships.

You may feel inclined to ask, what's the point of spending a few hours in church or praying daily when you're on top of the world? Those valuable hours could be applied to making more money. That is precisely what I used to think. But boy was I dead wrong. In good times and in bad, we all need spirituality. Taking a few minutes out of our day to thank the Lord and pray for your loved ones will truly enrich your life.

While it may not seem urgent to invite God into your life just yet, just keep in mind that emergencies and other unforeseen occurrences befall us all and when that happens, you will be crying and looking to Him for strength and help. You also never know when your last day on this Earth will be. He will help keep your priorities in check. He will help keep you balanced. He will help you keep your morals on the front burner and never forget them. He will help keep you honest. Embrace your faith and never put work before him and your family ever again.

Introducing some kind of daily worship to God doesn't have to be a grueling endeavor. It doesn't take long to say your prayers and acknowledge His presence throughout the day. I keep an extremely busy schedule with my *myriad* of activities. Yet, I find the time to pray while I'm driving, right after I have my first cup of coffee, and before falling asleep. Just a few minutes in the morning and more in the evening to give thanks for your existence, recite your prayers, and perhaps read your daily devotional is all it takes. We spend a lot more time on trivial things that don't really matter. Surely, we can all devote at least five minutes in the morning and another five in the evening to acknowledge our wonderful creator and thank Him for the many blessings He has bestowed upon us.

One of the best ways you can start each day is by reading a morning devotional and taking a few quiet moments to pray. There are several good books to help you with morning devotionals.

I happen to use the book titled *Jesus Calling* by Sarah Young. It only takes a few minutes to read that day's devotional and another minute to say your prayers. Is that too much to ask for to put God first in your life? I think not! *Treat every day equally* and make God number one.

If you are simply not the religious or spiritual type, at the very least maintain the morals and values that have been instilled in you by the people who raised you. Values are guiding principles. Without them, the world would be in constant chaos, more so than it already is. They are basic beliefs, the fundamental assumptions upon which all subsequent actions are based. As a whole, values define the personality and character of an individual. Values are the essence of an individual and provide guidelines by which to make consistent decisions. In reality, values are ideals that are indicative of one's vision of how the world should work. To be successful, one must adhere to personal and professional values.

The worst thing you can do is refuse to change the toxic behaviors that have turned you into an egotistical, selfish and uncaring workaholic. Once you place God before everything else in your life, personal and professional values should be easy to maintain. It will help you stop the lying, cheating and backstabbing. God's dominating presence in your life will help you to become more humble and cordial. You will be less selfish and more respectful of others. Maintaining your personal values can also lead to you becoming that extraordinary person who will go out of their way to help other people in need. Individuals who are steadfast in adhering to their personal values are more honest, sincere and caring. They also do what is right, regardless of any sort of personal sacrifices that is required of them.

Now let's talk about professional values. Someone who has deeply rooted professional values will avoid backstabbing people at work. Office politics run rampant throughout all organizations, and many employees have a bad habit of getting their co-workers in trouble for the sake of improving their professional careers. Climbing the management ladder can be exciting. With each new promotion comes a completely different set of challenges and opportunities. It is not that difficult to walk over people, and doing so usually comes with financial rewards. Don't renege on your morals, and you need to never bring yourself down to this level.

It's much more important to be respected by everyone around you than to compromise your values and destroy the reputation of others to satisfy your own agenda. Below are some examples practicing good professional values and the rewards that can be reaped:

- *Loyalty given/loyalty returned.* Be loyal to your friends, colleagues, and family. By this I mean being dedicated, considerate, and willing to make sacrifices for the good of all.
- *No surprises.* Never ambush your friends, colleagues, or associates. Differences of opinion should be worked out prior to any public meetings. It is your responsibility to make sure no one is taken by surprise. These kind of premeditated assaults lead to confusion, arguments and lack of trust.
- *Mutual respect.* Respect must be earned and cannot be assumed by force. Never embarrass anyone. Not only is it disrespectful, but it ruins relationships. Also, never make a commitment unless you can fulfill your obligation. It's very easy to lose respect for someone who never fulfills the commitments he or she makes. Treat others as you would like to be treated.
- *Honesty and candor.* It is surprisingly easy to be honest and at the same time be totally lacking in candor. If you need to be asked the precise question to elicit the required information then you are not doing your job efficiently. It is not enough to be honest in everything you say and do but, without being brutally frank, it is important to understand what is being asked and to answer with candor. Don't hoard information and don't beat around the bush either. Be objective and make sure what you say is supportable.
- *Integrity.* Your word should be absolutely and unwaveringly reliable. What people see and hear must be what you get. Walk the talk. It's painfully obvious when someone conducts their life in a negative way, but claims to do the exact opposite when in the company of others. It's better to admit to that you need to change than to try to convince yourself and others that "things are better than they appear." You will gain respect by being honest about your

shortcomings and your integrity will remain intact.

- *Professionalism.* This encompasses being objective, knowledgeable, competent, dependable, reliable, thorough, disciplined, and well-mannered.

In conclusion, you may not have time to attend church or worship God on a regular basis, but I believe if you hold fast to your values and keep the Lord first in your life you will continue to do the right things day after day.

Story: The Doctor

This story is dedicated to Dr. Mark Gray, a chiropractor in Sunnyvale, California. He is one of the finest individuals I have ever had the pleasure of knowing. In my opinion, Mark is the most caring and sincere human being in every aspect of life—personal and business—I have ever met. No one even comes close.

Mark is in his 50s, stands six feet tall, weighs about 200 pounds and has been exercising consistently for the past few decades. He's always had a wonderful physique. He has black hair and blue eyes, and is extremely personable and very good-looking. Mark always has a smile on his face and has never prejudged people. Now hold on, ladies: Mark has a beautiful wife named Gabrielle, and they have three lovely children. Gabrielle is like a daughter to me; in fact, I introduced Mark to Gabrielle. I wanted the absolute very best for her and she got it.

I met Mark at our health club; we occasionally worked out together. Our friendship flourished in the gym. My overly disciplined nature was motivation to him, and his values were an inspiration to me. It had all the makings of a beautiful friendship. Although I put my body through hell with my rigorous physical routine—at times exercising with excruciating pain—I would never visit with a doctor or chiropractor, even Mark. I never had the time. Besides, my discipline took me to a different level. My attitude was that I could beat any and all pain, and for almost two decades, that was the case. That is how foolish I was back in my early thirties.

On many occasions, he saw me working out while grimacing with pain. He urged me to come into his office for chiropractic treatment. Even though I considered him a friend, I still would not visit with him on a professional basis. Have you ever heard of the term "no pain, no gain?" I am sure who ever came up with that phrase was referring to the good type of pain—the soreness or exhausted feeling after a good workout. Ah, youth! I worked out with all types of pain, good and bad.

One day, I was in a severe car accident. My car was rear-ended. I was a physical wreck, but that did not cause me to miss work or working out. Three days after the accident, I was heading into the health club for my usual 5 A.M. workout. As I was getting out of my car I felt dizzy, so dizzy that I felt like I was walking sideways. It was a difficult morning; I barely got my workout in.

I was joking with Mark about the incident. Instead of laughing with me, he started to get mad at me and point-blank said to me, "I am taking you into my office for x-rays."

"No way," I said.

Mark became visibly upset and to make a long story short, he made me go. He also said there would be no charge—he genuinely wanted to help. I told him that I did not want to go to a chiropractor or doctor.

"Too bad. I'm taking you anyway," he made it clear.

What a truly remarkable person! The truth is Mark would have done this for anyone. When you feel pain, Mark feels pain. That's just the kind of human being he is. The bottom line is that if Mark did not have these values, regardless of my condition, I would not have gone into his office. I truly believed in him and put myself in his hands.

The treatments he provided not only got rid of the dizziness, but they also helped heal my whole body. I used to take aspirin at least once a week (more like 3-4 times a week) for twenty years because of the soreness in my knees, but not anymore. In my opinion Mark is a miracle worker, not only with his hands, but also, with his heart.

In this day and age, a guy like Mark can easily stray in more ways than one. Although he definitely has movie-star looks, a personality to match, and all the opportunity in the world—girls have asked him to go out (some have actually written to him)—he would never do it. Mark would never cheat on his wife. I think this is extraordinary. He just has these values like no other. I have seen some letters and so has Gabrielle. He hides nothing from her. Mark has incredible values as a human being. I would trust him with my life.

Spouse

Problem: Not investing quality time into relationships.

I failed miserably in my marriages. It wasn't until recently that I started to include every activity having to do with my personal life including family discussions into my evening routine and on my to-do list. Nowadays I keep it at the forefront—"out of sight and mind" is a recipe for failure. If only I had mastered the art of doing this a lot sooner, perhaps I'd still be married to my dream woman.

The most difficult aspect of maintaining a balanced lifestyle is when you have to interact with other humans on a daily basis—like your spouse for instance. On good days, everything is fine, but on the days when negative emotions just take over, then there is usually hell to pay. Those days filled with negativity can really derail your progress for hours or days at a time.

The key here is to be consistent. Communicating with your spouse and children about their day and not yours during dinner or movie time will certainly improve household relations. Whatever you decide to do—be consistent about it and give your spouse the attention he or she deserves. During this period, turn your mobile device off. Take it seriously. Studies have shown that divorce rates are 40 percent higher for marriages where a spouse is a workaholic. Studies have also shown that children of workaholics have higher anxiety and depression, even more so than children of alcoholic parents. My wakeup call was when I forgot my son's thirteenth birthday. That was really pathetic on my part. What a rude awakening that was, not to mention how deeply it hurt my son. Even though this major blunder happened more than 20 years ago, I am still paying the price of being the self-centered workaholic.

Family

Problem: Not spending quality time with your children.

After a lifetime of mistakes in this department, quality time with my children is sacred ground for me now. Due to my machine-like workaholic mannerisms, I destroyed two families. It wasn't my intention to do so. But when you're constantly neglecting your loved ones, what do you think is going to happen? Both my families loved me so much and they gave me repeated chances to make things right. All they wanted was to have their husband or father more present in their life. But I was too busy to tune into their needs. I was such a fool.

There is no greater gift on this planet than to have a loving family who truly cares for you and will be there for you regardless of the situation—good or bad. They will never turn their backs on you. I paid the ultimate price for ditching my family. Not only did I have to endure a very nasty divorce but my son hasn't spoken to me in ten years. He looks just like me, but he won't even give me the time of day. People say he will come around, but the prognosis doesn't look promising. Don't turn your back on your family. If you do, you're liable to end up alone like me.

Give your loved ones the proper attention before it's too late. Don't miss out on the most important years with your family. When you do find the time to spend with them, don't talk about work. Try listening to them for a chance. Who knows, you may just learn something new and current. If you have school-aged children, help them with their homework a few nights a week. These are the kinds of subtle things they are not likely to forget. Take the time to play with them also. Don't just buy them expensive toys and let them play by themselves, which in turn will allow you to work more. Set your work aside and play with them. It will make you feel good knowing you are fulfilling your parental obligations, and we all know how important that is.

Friends

Problem: No real time for friends.

My best friends' names are Mark, Rich and Howie. They are three of the best friends anyone could possibly hope to have. They are all sincere, genuine and trustworthy and have hearts of gold. I have helped them and they've helped me in return.

Mark is the chiropractor who I spoke about earlier. Rich is an Information Technology Manager. I used to mentor him in his career and also gave him tips on working out. It was fun watching him grow as a leader but Rich never lost sight of his family. He always kept them first. Howie is like a brother to me—actually much closer. Throughout the years of our friendship, we helped each other in the business world.

I've known each of these gentlemen for the past two decades, but for a ten-year period, I hardly called them. I was simply too busy being a workaholic. I actually abandoned them all for quite a few years. But once I took that hard fall, they were all there for me. So listen to the voice of experience and don't lose sight of your closest friends!

Realistically, after you institute a balanced lifestyle by including relationships and health as priorities, you're not going to have many cycles left over, if any, to nurture quality friendships. Spend quality time with only a few close friends. Now don't read this the wrong way. It's critical to have many friends, but realistically speaking, you just don't have the time. Pick and choose who you associate with in your spare time wisely.

When you find yourself amongst close friends, don't talk about work unless they are truly interested. However, most work-related topics that you can bring up will be irrelevant to your friends. Instead of leaning that way, talk about current events, sports, relationships, anything else. Nobody really cares about what's happening with your job.

Case Study

I had a male client whose main purpose in living was to cater to his girlfriend's needs. His entire existence was all about her. This guy put everything he had—all of his eggs—into one female basket. He didn't care about his current work situation and goals. He should have been worried about himself and the predicament he was in. He was in severe credit card debt and lived in a luxurious apartment that came with a high monthly price tag. My client was sixty pounds overweight and owned a broken-down car, yet he wanted to purchase a five-thousand-dollar engagement ring for his girlfriend. His plan was to pay for it in monthly installments. As well as buying an expensive rock for his girlfriend, he also wanted to get her a new car since hers was old and in really bad shape. It didn't seem to matter to him that he would be incurring even more debt. He was obsessed with his girlfriend and her needs and nothing else. I know, it's not very good...

He worked in IT as a database administrator. Although intelligent, he was unmotivated and lazy and did the bare minimum at work to get by. He started work at 9:00 A.M. and left exactly at 5:00 P.M., and not a minute more. Back then, in the dot-com boom, if you were only willing to work the bare minimum, then you didn't stand a chance in hell getting ahead. You also fell behind because the technology in that era was evolving so quickly that you really needed to keep abreast of the latest and greatest. Even today, there is *always* more work than available resources. My client was obsessed with only things that would directly impact his girlfriend at that given time. He didn't want to see the big picture and invest for the future. He was blinded by love or (who knows?) maybe just infatuated.

Unfortunately as with most relationships all is wonderful in the beginning. I'm not trying to be negative, but 8 out of 10 relationships typically go downhill after the honeymoon phase is over. Just like a healthaholic, he was a relataholic—okay, maybe that's not the best coinage, but I think you're getting the point. He needed a wakeup call before it was too late and his actions caused major damage to the rest of his life.

Changing the Mindset

There was only one way to make him change his ways. I had to paint a very ugly but true picture. Although things with his girlfriend were hunky-dory for the time being (most new relationships are wonderful in the beginning), chances were (based on actual statistics) that his relationship wasn't going to last. When it did fizzle out, he would be left with nothing but debt, no job, and poor health due to his obesity. It would be almost impossible for him to recover. As with all of my life coaching clients, I was very direct and to the point with him.

"You're a total mess—all you think about is your girlfriend day and night. Your mind is consumed by her, which hasn't allowed you to think clearly. Either we make some wholesale changes now or you're headed off of a very steep cliff." After letting him mull that over for a while, I continued scolding him, "If you lose your job tomorrow and have no income and no savings to your name, your relationship is going to go sour in a heartbeat. It's not only your financial situation, being obese, and having no motivation to improve your situation, you're playing Russian roulette with your health and career. You need to wake-up and leave Shangri-La for a bit before it becomes Hell for you."

The Cure

I knew from the get-go that the cure wasn't going to be easy. Many of us have been in his love-soaked shoes before—even myself, except I wasn't in debt, overweight or unmotivated. He had to eliminate his bad habits *quickly* or his fantasy world would eventually come tumbling down on him. If she truly loved him, then it stands to reason that she'd stick around and help him, although some of the changes would impact her in a big way.

It started with that five-thousand-dollar diamond ring he wanted to purchase. Instead of spending that much money on a ring, I suggested that his limit should be 1K. I made him see that there was no way he could go that much further into debt. He also needed to put in some extra hours at work to have a chance of getting promoted over the next year. He was intelligent enough to get a raise—he just needed to get motivated about his career. He needed to show management that he was a company man and willing to do whatever it takes to be recognized as a highly valued employee. Initiative is very important in IT because of the workload. Average performers typically don't survive.

He also needed to start managing his eating habits and exercise regularly to lose the weight. I put him on a strict regimen. For the time being he had to forget about buying his girlfriend a new car—that was totally out of the question. If and when they got married, then they could probably buy an inexpensive used car that would be more economical.

The most important thing for him was that he had to make himself the number one priority, not his girlfriend. Once he got his act together then he'd be able to focus equally on her. But unless he fixed himself first, he wasn't going to be good to anyone else. He was a disaster waiting to happen. To get out of the major rut he was in, he'd have to become disciplined and quickly. We established a new routine that revolved around his two new priorities *work* and *health*. We also set up goals for him with daily milestones to achieve. I would hold him accountable via telephone and Skype until his mind was trained and he could hold himself accountable. The plan worked like a charm and his girlfriend stayed with him throughout the transformation.

CHAPTER SEVEN

Being Disciplined

You're laser-focused and productive. Accomplishments are never-ending. You're a superstar. Congratulations: you get an A+ for doing so wonderfully. However, in your personal life, it's a whole different story. You fail miserably in relationships. You're overweight and do not pay enough attention to your family.

You know perfectly well that more balance is needed in your life. It's easy to use the word balance—who doesn't want more balance? However, to achieve and maintain true balance, you need to be disciplined in all three major areas of life equally. If not, you will find yourself falling back into the same old rut and a slave to one priority. Being disciplined has five main components:

1. Instituting structure (discussed below)
2. Prioritizing your life (discussed throughout the book)
3. Managing time (discussed throughout the book)
4. Holding yourself accountable (discussed below)
5. Seeking perfection (discussed below)

Each of these steps are thoroughly discussed in my book titled *Going from Undisciplined to Self-Mastery*.

A Powerful Combination—Self-Discipline Guru and Workaholic

In many instances workaholics were mentored by their parents during their teenage years—the underlying theme and message was pretty much the same with most parents: "Opportunities are out there—if you work hard the odds are you will be successful." The ones who listened and disciplined themselves to focus on their career were rewarded with success. Because they developed their self-discipline skills, they knew how to motivate themselves. That's a huge enabler for excelling in their job or business.

They were also very goal-oriented, efficient with time, strategic, and heavily focused on results. Being disciplined and having a work-hard mentality is quite a powerful combination—it can actually be deadly. Being reared to be disciplined in the corporate world was the key to success. Their only drawback is that they were focused on only their career or business and nothing else.

Assume for a moment if only they had applied their disciplined mannerisms into a healthy lifestyle and their relationships—heck, this book would never have been written. They wouldn't be in danger of taking that same hard fall that I did. They would actually have the kind of happy and balanced lifestyle that everyone seeks.

Challenge Yourself

Work-related activities always came naturally for me—the more the better. Whatever I touched turned to a pot of gold. Every ounce of energy was utilized in my IT career, publishing, writing books and consulting business. I had the key ingredient for success—I was disciplined. If you're disciplined, then challenge yourself to focus on your personal life before you destroy something that's more valuable than all the money you could possibly earn.

In general, workaholics are never afraid of challenges. Perhaps this describes you; then again, maybe not. What you need to ask yourself is: Are you afraid that becoming more disciplined in non-work related areas will take precious resources from your work? On the contrary, it will actually improve your overall performance. If everything is in harmony in your personal world, then your career will benefit more with all that added support from others.

If you're a workaholic, putting pressure on yourself to accomplish more is in your DNA. Nothing will change that. You're probably a Type A personality, like me. Focusing on your personal life (relationships and health) will not change that chemistry. Make your personal life a top priority—it has to be. Is there anything more important than a healthier lifestyle? If you have a spouse and children, be motivated by the thought of spending quality time together. One of the greatest joys in life is witnessing your children grow up into wonderful, caring, and responsible adults before your very eyes.

On the other side of the fence, if you exercise consistently, you will have more energy and stamina. If you have a good relationship with your spouse and God, it will make your life that much more meaningful and productive. Look at your personal life as an enabler for your career, not a hindrance. How many times have you and your significant other been in a heated argument before going to bed and it put a halt to your productivity the next day? Be proactive; don't take your personal life for granted like I did for so many years. Challenge yourself every day to excel in your career, health, and relationships equally.

It's okay to add more to your already full plate—*albeit slowly.* Yes, you're reading this correctly. Allow me to explain. You are already confident and new challenges turn you on. You have a *whatever-it-takes* attitude and you can take on anything—right? Sure, in your professional world. But what you are not fully grasping is that's your comfort zone. In the other two major areas of your life, not so much. You rarely have time and you know it. When those highly stressful projects require your undivided attention, you find yourself working 15+-hour days and nights. The other areas quickly fall by the wayside. This gives you the perfect excuse for not dealing with any aspect of your personal life—especially exercising.

Structure

Being structured is the foundation of success for organizations and individuals. The more structured you are, the more efficient you become. There is no disputing this. If you ask most successful people and organizations, they will tell you their high productivity levels stem from being structured.

To take on additional activities (by including your personal life as a priority), you will need to be more structured than ever. You don't have time as it is, so what makes you think you can take on activities related to your personal life and still be successful in your career? It's doable—trust me, it's doable. Will there be additional sacrifice on your part? You can count on it. I'd be lying through my teeth if I said there wouldn't be. Nothing this rewarding comes without a price tag. However, the overall cost is minimal. There are several key actions you need to take to maintain structure:

1. Be organized
2. Follow an efficient routine rigorously
3. Follow your to-do list
4. Treat every day equally
5. Be punctual

Below are the details behind these important components except for *being punctual*. As for being punctual, just do it! Don't disrespect others and waste their time by being late.

With a structured lifestyle, you will gain back some of those precious minutes you currently throw away every day on nonsense. Those minutes will add up to hours by week's end. Structure will make your life easier to manage. It's not only children who thrive in a structured environment; adults function best with one also.

Be Organized

Every area in your life needs to be organized, whether it's your home, car, office, computer, desk drawers, closet, garage or anything else. You name it—organize it! Being unorganized wastes precious cycles of time, which you don't have. The more organized you are, the more productive you will be. The same principle also applies to your mind.

Don't clutter your mind with nonsense. Start out with a blank slate every morning. All of your activities for the day ahead should have been documented on your to-do list the night before. That leaves your mind free to strategize your next career move and foster and strengthen relationships. Structure begins and ends with organizing every aspect of your life.

Establish and Adhere to a Routine that Promotes Balance

Having an efficient routine, especially in the morning, will be the key enabler for success. Your morning routine should be the catalyst that provides the motivation and energy for the rest of your day. It's about waking up with a purpose—to kick butt and accomplish something every day of the year.

I can't stress enough just how crucial it is to get the day started on a high note. It's also important to make sure that your routine encapsulates all three of your priorities. For example, your exercise routine takes care of one priority. Your prayers and family obligations scheduled throughout the late afternoon and evening will support another priority. And you know what comes next. I certainly don't have to remind a workaholic to focus on work. That comes naturally.

The evening routine is important too. Be sure to schedule time to bond with your spouse and children. You might be surprised how working together as a family to get the household chores done like clearing the table, washing dishes, and taking out the garbage can actually bring you closer together. You will also want to make it a point to shut down and unwind at a decent hour so that you get ample sleep. In the morning, you want to feel refreshed and not overly tired. Helping your spouse out, regardless of how tired you may be, is a surefire way to keep you out of the doghouse. Remember, they probably had a long day as well.

Before calling it a night, pick out your clothes for the next day, have your to-do list ready, make a lunch and organize your briefcase for work. All these things should be done in the evening, not in the morning. This way you won't have to think when getting out of bed—just execute. For me, my morning routine involves getting the coffee going, looking at email, saying my prayers, reading my daily devotional, going to the bathroom and getting to the gym. When I get back home, I take a shower and get to the office. Before the clock strikes noon, I make sure two very important priorities in my life have been addressed: my health and personal relationship with God.

Follow Your To-Do List
Begin living a balanced lifestyle by incorporating non work-related activities on your to-do list. Don't just pay lip service by saying you will—that doesn't work. Workaholics can talk a heck of a good game and can easily convince themselves that nothing trumps work. Document all professional, personal and spiritual tasks, obligations and activities on your to-do list. This includes

very important spiritual obligations like your daily prayers, bible readings, going to Church, and any other faith-based practices. All activities that are associated with your new priorities should be on your to-do list.

I write down all my pending activities the night before. You name it—it should be on that list. Follow it and maintain it rigorously. Train your mind by focusing on those documented activities daily, constantly looking at that list and living your life by it. This is the *only* way to ensure balance in your life. If it's not on your to-do list, it's out of sight and out of mind.

Make sure to document all commitments with your spouse or significant other including but not limited to date nights, taking the garbage out, washing dishes, picking up the kids from school, watching a movie together, and so on. It's crucial to set boundaries between your personal and professional world. Don't forget setting time aside for your personal well-being. Carve out some time to meditate, read, exercise, listen to music, engage in sports, and maintain friendships. Even the simplest things are often overlooked when you're a real workaholic, like trimming your fingernails. For me, it was shaving. You heard right, shaving was one of those pending activities that had to be on my to-do list or it wouldn't get done until my beard was out of control and my wife had to yell at me. Take those small baby steps by documenting the simplest of non-work-related activities to introduce true change into your life.

Try your best to create your to-do list each evening so you can hit the ground running as soon as the sun rises. You shouldn't be making out your to-do list in the morning. By then, it's really too late. Once it's been completed, focus on the items on the list and maintain it throughout the day. As new personal or professional obligations arise, add or delete them from the list.

I am programmed to look at my to-do list throughout the day and into the evening. I used to only write down work-related activities 24x7. Well, guess what I saw day and night? It was a form of brainwashing I tell you. I was only looking at work-related tasks and obligations that consumed every minute I had. There was nothing on my list reserved for faith or family. It was easy to get sucked into this ugly routine.

Workaholics are fairly disciplined creatures, but usually in only one area. When it comes to their work, they tend to be extremely goal-oriented, focused, self-motivated, and operate with a sense of urgency. They also manage their resources effectively. That new balanced life starts with a thorough, consistently utilized and maintained to-do list and then holding yourself accountable to follow through.

Treating Every Day Equally

"What exactly does that mean? I don't want to treat weekends and holidays the same as every day. I need to relax and throw my structure out the door every once in a while."

Let me explain—you wake up with a purpose and adhere to your routine seven days a week. Your weekend or holiday routine could certainly be modified without having any major repercussions to your new structured lifestyle. Regardless of how you decide to change things up, your daily routine should always have that one constant—some sort of exercise. Get the day started by doing something good for you. Whether it's just walking around the block or cleaning the apartment, partake in some sort of physical activity first. Of course your modified version for weekends and holidays could be as simple as taking a walk on the beach or around the mall. All of that can be considered exercise. The important thing is to be consistent day in and day out. Treat every day equally and before you know it, you'll be living a well-balanced life.

My daily routine has been the same for many years. Since I sleep a whole lot less than my family, I typically wake up in the wee hours of the morning and then proceed to go through my usual aforementioned regimen. I manage to do all these things before anyone in my household wakes up. For me, that's *treating every day equally*.

Accountability

One of the most difficult things to do consistently is holding yourself accountable to all of your daily tasks, projects and obligations on your to-do list, to ensure balance is achieved. This cannot be a part-time effort. I can't stress that enough.

This is where the rubber meets the road. You can have the perfect roadmap, the best business or marketing plan, but what good is a roadmap with specific action items and due dates if you can't hold yourself accountable in the end? The most effective way to hold yourself accountable is to train your mind to do so automatically. Although I mentioned it earlier in this chapter, it's important to know that there is a great deal of effort that goes into training your mind. If not done properly, you will never hold yourself accountable consistently. In *Going from Undisciplined to Self-Mastery*, I go into considerable detail on what accountability is, how you attain it by training your mind and the end results.

Never Be Complacent

You should always try to be more productive, especially when you know there will always be more work to do than there are resources in a day. Strategize on how you can be more efficient from the time you wake up until it's time for bed. There's always room for improvement. Never be satisfied: constantly seek perfection and to accomplish more. The more you accomplish in a 24-hour period the more satisfied you'll be at the end of the day. The secret is to stay hungry and never be completely satisfied. The best thing you can do is to keep strategizing to be more efficient and eventually take on more. The more you accomplish, the hungrier you will be, and complete satisfaction will be a figment of your imagination.

It's important not to become a workaholic in pursuit of your many accomplishments. No one lying on their deathbed regrets not having spent more time at work. The true measure of a person's success and happiness is their emotional, physical and psychological well-being. What I'm saying is to never be satisfied with the level of efficiency and happiness you've attained. There are always areas in our lives that need attention to keep the balance consistent. Being happy in all aspects of your life is the mother of all accomplishments. Don't settle. If you must, remember to always settle for more.

BONUS SECTION

Managing Sleep Optimally

Problems:

- *Not enough hours in the day to effectively manage all three priorities.*

- *Not getting quality sleep.*

- *Not getting enough sleep.*

- *Spending too much time lounging around in bed.*

- *Not waking up with a purpose.*

Solution: Don't take sleep for granted—manage it.

I've written this bonus section for those of you who have a problem of sleeping too much or not getting sufficient quality sleep. Consider the following tips on how to sleep less while improving the quality of your sleep.

One of the first things you will want to do is stop working a few hours before hitting the sack. If you typically go to sleep around 11 P.M. then stop responding to email by 9:00 P.M. Take a shower, relax, read a book or watch some television just to unwind.

Try and get six to seven hours of quality sleep and then get out of bed promptly. Don't lounge around continuously hitting the snooze button. That is precisely how many people end up squandering up to thirty minutes per day.

As a workaholic, you want to sleep less, but you're concerned that your cognitive abilities will suffer greatly if you fail to get enough beauty rest. So, what do you do? What is the right answer? One course of action is to increase the quality of your sleep while also decreasing the amount of time you sleep.

Years ago, I was so obsessed about achieving goals and not wanting to waste time that I started experimenting with reducing my amount of sleep. To me sleep was a complete waste of time. I was fortunate in that despite getting minimal sleep, I still maintained a healthy lifestyle. I didn't drink, smoke, do drugs, exercised seven days a week and ate healthy.

I tackled the problem by reducing the amount I slept by half an hour every ten days. I also would pace myself during the day so that I did brain-intensive activities when I was most alert, which was in the morning before lunch. I also performed hypnosis on myself and somehow convinced my mind that I didn't need much sleep to function normally. Because of my physical makeup, I was able to get my body used to functioning on four hours of sleep a night. I started doing this four decades ago!

Here comes my legal disclaimer:

I am not a medical doctor. I am merely offering my own life experience as information for you. I do NOT recommend you sleep only four hours a day.

I do realize that in these days of intense demand on time, many people are trying to find more hours in the day. I did some intensive research on the subject of sleep, both on improving the quality of sleep and reducing the amount of hours I slept.

As a result of my research findings, please consider the following suggestions and see if by implementing some of them you can improve the quality of your sleep and reduce the amount of hours. I would be interested in hearing of your experiences.

What if you don't want to reduce the amount of hours you sleep? By following these tips on how to improve the quality of your sleep, you will have more energy and be more productive during the time you are awake.

Never mind that you spend almost a third of your life asleep. If you want to get creative, you can experiment with lucid dreaming or learning while you sleep. So let's learn more about this subject.

What is Sleep?

Sleep is the time when your brain and nervous system **rejuvenates** itself. It is also the time your body repairs itself and your spirit connects to higher levels. Here are some fascinating sleep facts.

- Your body has an internal 24-hour clock which controls your **circadian rhythm.** This periodic rise and drop in body temperature tells our mind when to feel tired and when to feel more awake. As body temperature rises, we tend to feel more awake and our brain waves are usually higher. As body temperature drops, we tend to feel more lethargic, tired, and lazy—this is a big cue for our minds to lower brain waves.
- Most adult humans are naturally wired for sleeping twice every 24-hour period—a 6-to-7-hour nocturnal rest with a 20 to 60 minute siesta in the afternoon.
- One of the greatest expenditures of energy in the body is from **digestion of food.** Large amounts of blood flow are directed toward the digestive system after a large meal. This means less blood flow, thus less energy, available for the brain. Low blood flow in the brain during sleep means poor sleep quality, since the brain conducts all sleep processes. So eat light in the evening.
- Your brain cycles through the different stages of sleep, oscillating between deep sleep and light/REM sleep in a period of about 90 minutes.

- Darker sleep increases melatonin, which increases sleep quality and promotes good health.
- Deep sleep is very important for cognitive performance. A lot of "neural housecleaning" occurs during deep sleep, which makes it important for mood, performance, motor skills, productivity, and creativity.
- During deep sleep your **cerebral cortex**—the conscious part of your brain—nearly shuts off. Neural activity in the cerebral cortex break down into little islands that can't talk to one another.
- If you go to sleep stressed out, your mind and brain will be attempting to deal with the stress and this will act as a strain and you won't get quality sleep.
- If you currently spend less than an hour getting high-intensity light, you're suffering from **light deprivation! Remember, for your eyes,** spending the day indoors is equivalent to spending it in total darkness. The more "darkness" you expose yourself to during the day, the poorer the sleep you'll receive in return.
- Your body temperature drops after a hot bath in a way that mimics, in part, what happens as you fall asleep.
- The tiniest amount of light can disrupt circadian rhythm and your pineal gland's production of melatonin and serotonin. **LEDs** from alarm clocks and computers, although dim, actually do have a measurable effect on sleep quality.
- The wake-up process occurs via increased blood flow to the brain, which is facilitated by the stress hormones ACTH and cortisol. By anticipating a wake-up time, we set our internal alarm clock. When it arrives, the brain signals the pituitary and adrenal glands to spike ACTH and cortisol. This causes you to wake up.
- Meditation improves sleep quality. It reduces interruptions to deep sleep. It does this by reducing cortisol levels during the day. Cortisol is what destroys sleep quality.
- Our brains thrive on automation.
- Our brain runs on habits.
- **EMF** stands for *electro-magnetic field.* EMFs are released by electronic appliances present within your sleeping environment. EMFs are known to disrupt the pineal

gland and interfere with the production of melatonin and serotonin, which are essential in promoting good sleeping patterns.

- Our body's natural biological clock has been thrown out of balance because of modern electricity and lighting. Biologically, the body wants to go to sleep around 10:00 P.M. and wake up around sunrise.

Things You Can Do During the Day that Will Improve Your Sleep at Night

- Exercise
- Get daily sunlight
- Eat a healthy diet with organic fruits and vegetables
- Stay away from junk food and processed food
- Take a power nap
- Meditate
- Maintain a positive attitude
- Consume flaxseed oil
- Make sure you're regular
- Drink lots of water

Things to Avoid in the Evening

- Nicotine or other stimulants
- Arguments
- Heavy meals
- Watching the news
- Heavy exercise
- Anything upsetting

Before Going to Sleep:

- De-stress, which improves the quality of your sleep
- Practice EFT on any distressing things that occurred during the day (EFT stands for Emotional Freedom Technique, find out how to do this at www.emofree.com, an easy to use de-stressing technique)
- Make a list of the things you need to do the next day
- Practice deep rhythmic breathing
- Think of five things you are grateful for
- Forgive the people who upset you that day

- Take a warm bath (adding Epsom salts and lavender oil or sea salt)
- Drink soothing herbal tea (I recommend Sleepy-Time brand)
- Take melatonin
- Ingest magnesium
- Do light stretches
- Take some probiotics such as yogurt or kefir

Make Your Bedroom a Sanctuary
- Find sheets that feel good on your skin
- Find colors that comfort you
- Have a picture you enjoy looking at
- Reduce noise and light
- Remove EMF fields such as TV, clock radios and cable boxes
- Make the space really dark
- Wear a sleep mask
- Listen to soothing music
- Turn down your thermostat to a cool temperature
- Get an ionizer or humidifier to improve the air quality of your bedroom
- Buy a comfortable mattress
- Visualize a beautiful place that you can go to for relaxation and peace

Start Winding Down an Hour or Two Before Going to Bed
- Take time for yourself
- Eat a light high-protein snack
- Decrease your intake of liquids
- Read
- Do something that makes you happy
- Create a routine

Suggestions for Waking Up
- Establish a routine
- Invest in a light box that gradually increases the light
- Get some uplifting music
- Do some stretches

- Drink as much water as you can
- The juice of a lemon and some honey with water
- Eat some fruit

Ridding Yourself of False Beliefs

You might have some strange ideas about the amount of sleep that you need, things your parents or friends might have told you.

A useful idea is to purge yourself of these unproven beliefs as they could interfere with your efforts to change your lifestyle. Make a list of all the different biased things people have said or you have read or seen on TV concerning the subject of sleep.

Talk to Yourself about the Value of Time

Treat time as if it were your most valuable resource, which it is. Grab onto the idea of really focusing on what you are doing and when you are doing it so that you're devoting all of your attention to one thing. So if you are sleeping, you are fully and completely sleeping. If you are spending time with your family, then fully enjoy the moment. If you are eating, then only eat and really taste your food. Ponder on the value of time.

Sleep Affirmations to Say to Yourself a Few Times a Day

- I choose to fall asleep easily.
- I enjoy deep refreshing sleep that fully rejuvenates me.
- I dream creatively.
- I need less and less sleep to feel fully refreshed.
- Get out of bed promptly.
- I will sleep only _ hours a night.

A way to get your body used to sleeping less is start implementing as many of the above suggestions as possible, while reducing the time that you sleep a half hour at a time. You need to stay at the reduced level for ten days at least, before reducing it by another thirty minutes.

What to Do if You Get Foggy or Tired During the Day

- Take a power nap of twenty minutes
- Drink vinegar and honey with your water to alkalize your body

- Take antioxidants (vitamin C, vitamin E, alpha-lipoic acid, etc.)
- Increase your mineral intake (dried fruits, seaweed, etc.)
- Practice deep breathing
- Do light stretching
- Go to that special place in your mind that makes you happy
- Drink water with a splash of lemon
- Go for a short walk, really noticing things around you
- Have some green tea (Matcha tea)
- Take some ginseng

So there you have it; a smorgasbord of suggestions to try. Sweet dreams!

THE HARRIS KERN STORY

There was a time, not so long ago, that I found myself on top of the world—highly successful and growing my legacy by leaps and bounds. I had it all planned out. My children and the love of my life were going to be the beneficiaries of more than just a hefty bank account. They would inherit prime real estate property and multiple businesses. They would also have a vast collection of books I authored in the family library and vivid photographs on the mantle to remember me by. In my mind, they would continue to abide by the morals their mother and I instilled in them. I also assumed they would adhere to the same top three priorities that I did and continue to develop their self-discipline so they'd wake up every morning for the rest of their lives with a purpose. Just like their dear old dad, I wanted them to accomplish as much as possible every day. Faith, balance and discipline would always be the catalyst for their own success.

Looking back over my 60 years of existence, there were plenty of major accomplishments to write home about. One of the things I'm most proud of is the fact that at age 16, I purchased, in cash, a brand spanking new car and paid for my own insurance. My workaholic mannerisms and tendencies manifested themselves at an early age. At the age of 13, I threw myself into the labor market with a vengeance. I wanted money and truckloads of it—quickly, especially after having netted approximately $700.00 in cash, checks and bonds at my *bar mitzvah* in 1967.

To appease my never-ending hunger for money, I worked multiple jobs after school and on the weekends. There was no job big or small that I wouldn't do; yard work, babysitting, delivering newspapers, filing brochures at a travel agency. At one time, I even worked at an auto junkyard pulling batteries from old clunkers. It was a dirty and dangerous job, but someone had to do it. I'll never forget the day that I pulled out a battery from a car right before it was being hoisted up for demolition. As I stood there and watched it being lifted by a crane, a large rattlesnake fell out and scared the crap out of me. That was the straw that broke the camel's back. I never went back after that.

These jobs were all performed between the ages of 13 to 16, with 100 percent of the income being deposited into my savings account. It was the only way I could purchase a new car by my 16th birthday. Growing up, I was mentored to be frugal and save money. My parents always used to tell me, "Never purchase small insignificant items like records, beer, media paraphernalia, and knickknacks at the mall. Forget all about the latest craze and always eat at home." Their sound advice has served me well throughout my entire life.

While other teenage boys were busy scamming for girls or getting into all kinds of trouble, I had already entered the corporate world. I was only 18 years old when I accepted an entry-level position in the Information Technology (IT) department of a large manufacturing company. Back in 1972, IT was referred to as data processing and shortly thereafter as Management Information Systems (MIS). Removing the carbon sheets from computer-generated printouts wasn't exactly a glamorous job, but it was the proverbial *foot in the door* that I needed to gain full admittance into the very exciting world of technology.

It was a full-time job, but I completed my duties in approximately five hours of my day. The rest of it was spent helping out in other departments—learning, growing and striving to get on management's radar screen as a quick learner, efficient, and someone with a ton of initiative. My goal was to be promoted out of that function—the sooner, the better. I had bigger fish to fry. I knew the faster I climbed the corporate ladder the sooner I would make the big bucks.

As long as I live, I'll never forget what my dad said to me at an early age. "Son, always save for the big stuff. If you rent an apartment or house it's like flushing your hard-earned money down the toilet." Needless to say, I took these words to heart. Living on my own became a goal of mine, one that turned into reality at the age of 19, when I purchased a home in the San Francisco Bay Area.

My life changed drastically when I bought my first home without any financial help from anyone. It was a two-bedroom townhome about 15 minutes south of San Francisco. I was scared to death of getting tied down to a mortgage at such a young age—it was nerve-racking to say the least. However, it was a fairly conservative strategy, putting down a larger down payment of 20 percent so the monthly payments wouldn't strap me down. Investing in property at an early age was one of my smartest undertakings. The only risk was the location, due to the weather in that area—it wasn't very good, typically cooler than the rest of the Bay Area due to the constant fog, which made home prices a bit more reasonable and the perfect starter home. After two years, I sold it for a nice profit and moved to a much nicer neighborhood. After dabbling in real estate, I turned my focus to muscle cars. There were millions of nice muscle cars out there, but I wanted to have so much more than just another fancy hot rod. What I yearned for was something wholly unique that would win "Best of Class" at all the premier car shows in the U.S. At the age of 21, I had my muscle car and matching speedboat, each with a maroon-with-flames paint job.

Both were showcased at the granddaddy of all car shows in Oakland, California. They won the top prize—best of show. I named the boat *Dirty Harry* and the car *Sano SS*. Winning "Best of Show" was the ultimate honor for the combo… until I received a phone call from *Hot Rod Magazine* a few weeks later. A representative saw the car and boat at the car show and wanted to feature them in one of the magazine's summer issues. Wow, what a great feeling when it hit newsstands and stores in July of 1975! I'll never forget driving my award-winning muscle car to the lakes throughout California with matching speed boat in tow to water-ski. I made quite a spectacle cruising on the streets and highways.

Early in my career, I knew that management was the right path to take. It was where the big bucks were, along with once-in-a-lifetime opportunities and character-building challenges. Having good communication skills, always thinking strategically, possessing excellent leadership skills and being passionate about developing a highly efficient organization was my true calling. At the age of 23, I was promoted to my first management position. From that point on, I climbed the corporate ladder at nearly a record-setting pace and went on to become Vice President of IT in my early thirties.

By the time I reached my 38th birthday in 1992, I was financially set —*a multi-millionaire*. One million dollars' worth of equity in property and another cool million in cash constituted success for me, at the time. I invested wisely—mostly in property—worked hard, and never put all my eggs in one basket. I made it a point to make sure there was always a steady stream of income coming in from several small consulting firms just in case that big *reduction in force* (RIF) happened.

In 1982, my corporate job of 10 years ended abruptly—everyone was given a pink slip, including yours truly. Being unemployed for the first time in my professional life was downright scary, but having a healthy savings account and multiple sources of income to pay the mortgage and living expenses for approximately two years eased the burden considerably. In a matter of a few months, I was recruited by a large Japanese electronics company in Silicon Valley.

Once I got back into the corporate world, my goal was for the name Harris Kern to become synonymous with IT and self-discipline. At the time, based on my research, there were many IT one-book wonders. But that wasn't going to cut the mustard with me. I wanted an impressive bio that would clearly stand apart from the pack, which could also be used as my resume, one that would open up any door for me.

My first IT-related book was published in 1994 by Prentice Hall and it quickly became a best-seller. Shortly thereafter, the president of Prentice Hall called to congratulate me and he asked me, "When are you going to write another book?" Little did he know that my mind was already actively strategizing to write a series of IT management how-to books.

After that, I was invited to attend a conference in 1997, which was facilitated by Prentice Hall in San Diego, California. All of the top-level publishing executives were in attendance, including my executive editor and his boss. My objective was to get my own imprint of books named Harris Kern's Enterprise Computing Institute. I presented my plan to them with conviction and they agreed. Over the next few weeks we worked out the contractual issues. The imprint published its first book in the series in 1997. It worked flawlessly with dozens of new books being published under my imprint on a regular basis. Overall, I published more than 40 books with Prentice Hall and a few other publishers as well. On the Richter scale of personal success, I considered myself to be a rock star as an IT management consultant, motivational speaker, and life coach.

Throughout my career, I easily logged more than four million air miles. I traveled the globe several times over, speaking on the subject of building world-class organizations and how to improve productivity by being disciplined. There were many more accomplishments, but I think you've gotten a pretty good grasp of the level of success I enjoyed. Let's just say that I was riding high. It was a continuous high, an addictive feeling like no other. In retrospect, it was like living in a bubble that could never burst no matter what sharp obstacles came its way. I often felt invincible, stronger than a team of gladiators. That's right, my workaholic habits took me all the way to the moon, but in time, I eventually came crashing down to the bottom of the ocean.

Looking back to when I was in my twenties and thirties, as much as it pains me to say it, I was a big f***ing jerk. (BFJ) The only reason I got away with it is because I was a highly successful BFJ. Then the big crash came—Mr. BFJ got what he deserved.

My rude awakening occurred when I lost my family. One day I woke up and smelled the coffee. The woman I loved more than life itself walked out of my life and took my stepchildren with her. Recently, I wrote a book titled *Going from Undisciplined to Self-Mastery* and the picture on the front cover features a samurai sword with a single, breathtaking white lily draped over it. The reason for the lily is because that had always been my ex-wife's favorite flower. Throughout our entire relationship and marriage, I was the strong one and my ex-wife was the beautiful and delicate one. Suddenly, all the happiness in my life was gone and it seemed like death was near and calling my name.

Further down, I will describe in detail how I fought back. Through the grace of God, help from a few friends, a brand new life strategy, and unwavering self-discipline skills, I was able to regain my mojo. Crawling my way up from the pit of despair I had dug for myself meant many dark moments. For the first time in my life, I was alone day and night. But what I didn't realize then was that Jesus Christ had never left my side the entire time. However, the physical loneliness, coupled with so many conflicting emotions, were eating me alive, little by little. At least twice a week, I felt severe numbness all over my body. Sometimes it was so overwhelming that the agonizing feeling lasted the entire day.

On many occasions I wanted to purchase a gun to take the easy way out. I never told my business partner, co-author and close friend Leticia about this—it would have freaked her out. I also only slept two to three hours a night, which she knew and scolded me about frequently.

Due to the depression, health problems began to crop up more frequently. I had daily headaches, high blood pressure, anxiety and numbness on the left side of my body in specific areas. My emotional well-being and physical state were, to put it mildly, not very good. With all those issues on top of the number one killer of them all, being *alone*, I was a mess. But I fought back, with some help.

My Awakening

In hindsight, I can honestly say it was one of the most grueling 48-hour periods of my life. Despite several futile attempts to self-medicate by working round the clock, I hit rock bottom and succumbed to my loneliness. Except for dozing off for a few minutes here and there, I hardly slept. To keep my stomach from growling so loudly, I ate a few light snacks. My aching loneliness was driving me crazy and preventing me from functioning as a normal human being. Although I had plenty of work to do and I typically go to the gym seven days a week, it all came to an abrupt halt. I was down and out like I'd never been before. I didn't just have "the blues;" I was majorly depressed. The lights were on but nobody was home. Up until then, I had experienced many bouts of depression, especially after my divorce, but I'll never forget those critical 48 hours: March 27th and 28th of 2014.

Each bout of depression had gotten worse over the past two years since my divorce, but this time I was in an even deeper pit. My depression had spiraled out of control and coupled with my high blood pressure, which I never took medication for, I actually could sense that something was going terribly wrong. I felt dizzy and I couldn't get off the couch. The loneliness and severe depression was taking me to a whole different place. I just laid on the couch and did nothing (around the clock) except pray and cry. I was a genuine basket case. I missed my wife and family so much. That day nearly marked the two-year anniversary of my divorce. There I was at age 60, completely withering away minute by minute in a spacious six-bedroom home. My biggest fear in life had reared its ugly head to bite me where it most hurt—I was alone.

Two years prior to that day, my wife had filed for divorce and it had destroyed me in every way imaginable. I loved her then and with the passing of time nothing has changed. I continue to love her as if she was still my wife and never left my side. The way I feel is not going to change until the day I die. Nowadays, my home is designed and set up exactly as if my family was still living with me. Throughout the house, wedding and travel pictures are mounted on the wall. A collection of cards I gave my wife on momentous occasions are spread throughout the house as well. I've decorated every room with the furniture we purchased together when we were once a happily married couple. I even laid out her PJs as if she was still sleeping on her side of the bed every night. Weird, I know— even stranger to write about it, but that's how much I love my wife.

As a monument of my love for her, I made a promise to myself. I promised that I would die with her being the last woman I will ever love in my heart. Keeping this promise means a lot to me— regardless of the pain and suffering I must continue to endure. I also felt that the entire divorce was a farce. During the span of our marriage, I had never broken any of the Ten Commandments, certainly not the one about adultery. Did I make mistakes? I'm human just like everyone else. Were they bad? Yes, they were. Were they enough to initiate divorce proceedings over? No.

I am still hopeful that one day she will see it in her heart to accept me back as her husband. She's my Puerto Rican Goddess and has always been the woman of my dreams. She has a wonderful heart and personality.

Prior to March 27, 2014, I was surviving on memories alone, but just barely. I knew perfectly well that I was being childish. Down deep, I also realized that I was intentionally destroying myself. I knew that she had let me go and gone on with her life, but it didn't matter to me. I couldn't change the feelings in my heart even if I wanted to. Sure, I knew that living on memories alone was unhealthy and it oftentimes brought me to my knees, but I didn't care. Perhaps I was a foolish old man who just loved his wife too much. I was losing it mentally and physically. I honestly didn't think I would make it another 24 hours and I didn't care. At this juncture, I had absolutely nothing to live for.

Then my Guardian Angels came out of nowhere. First it was an old priest friend of mine from Atlanta who reached out to me. There was a time I used to commute from my home in Dallas to Atlanta on business. I met Donald Stewart when I was in the process of going through my divorce. He actually helped me through some really difficult times. Out of the blue, after nearly six months of not hearing from him, on the evening of March 28th he called to lift my spirits. He prayed and prayed hard for me.

Then, as if on cue, my other Guardian Angel, Leticia Gomez, my literary agent, called and heard the depression in my voice. It took her but a few seconds to sense that my loneliness had taken me to a place I shouldn't be. Several times before, she had traveled down that road with me. She could always tell when I was depressed even though I never admitted it. Some days were worse than others. On this particular day, knowing how stubborn I could be, she was scared to death for me. So she did what she does best—prayed and found ways to break through that stubbornness of mine.

I wasn't really in the mood to talk so I cut the conversation short. After she hung up, I didn't hear from her for several hours. Then she sent a text to my number instructing me to read several emails she had written ASAP. Again, I really wasn't in the mood, but I complied with her request, because I respect her as a business partner and friend. She has a very caring demeanor and a heart of gold besides being a genius.

What transpired next was truly a miracle, all the emails she had written and sent impacted me deeply. This one in particular really *woke* up the human being inside of me that had been sleeping for so long:

After making the Earth, God decided to create human beings to inhabit it forever. The Bible tells us he created Adam out of dust from the ground. Now there's no telling how long Adam existed alone in the Garden of Eden before God decided to give him a female companion. It could have been hundreds and hundreds of years that Adam was alone, which goes to show that man can exist without female companionship. But being the loving Father that he is, God saw it was not good for man to continue alone so while Adam slept he took one of his ribs and out of that created Eve to enhance his life.

Upon waking from a deep sleep, Adam had it all: a beautiful home, a gorgeous trophy wife at his side, perfect health and youthful vigor. He had the prospect of living forever without suffering. However, that all changed one day when Satan the Devil tricked Eve into disobeying God by eating the forbidden fruit from the "Tree of Life." Obviously Satan knew it would be easier to deceive Eve because she was not a direct creation of God and this is why he targeted her first. But in reality, Adam proved to be the weaker of the two. After Eve had already sinned and approached Adam to offer him a bite of the fruit, the smart thing for him to do would have been to refuse the offering. But he did not. Instead of exercising his headship over the woman, he gave in to her and, in doing so, condemned humanity. Since we are all descendants of Adam and Eve, this is the reason that we grow old and die.

Now think for a moment about how things might have turned out differently if only Adam had been strong enough to stand his ground and obey God instead of "his woman." Surely had he remained loyal, in time, God would have given him another woman to replace Eve. Harris, in a way, you are in the same predicament that Adam was in long ago. You have the chance to live for yourself, be happy, and have a close, personal relationship with God. Think about it, God knows you are drowning in a sea of loneliness but He has thrown you a life preserver. He has already sent you a special friend to help you get through this harrowing chapter of your life. And if you ask me, he has sent you a very good one. So, stop punishing yourself and hold on to the life preserver God has sent you until you are strong enough to swim on your own again.

After reading this spiritual reflection, I woke up in a BIG way. It was almost as if a bolt of lightning went through my system and shocked me back to life with an intensity I had never felt before. I instantly filled up with boundless energy and my adrenalin began to flow like a river. I called Leticia immediately and she could tell I had come back from the dead. Leticia (via God) saved my life. The message in this email hit me like a ton of bricks—I wasn't alone. God never leaves our side. As it turned out, I had the best companion in the Universe: God.

With God at the helm, ensuring my values were adhered to daily, and my angels by my side, I rebuilt, stronger and better than ever before, using my disciplined mannerisms to live a more balanced lifestyle. That is my story: the ultimate *(machine-like)* workaholic who fell hard but who fought back by focusing on my career, health and relationships to ensure they ALWAYS received equal billing.

ABOUT THE AUTHOR

Harris Kern is one of the world's leading organization (www. disciplinetheorganization.com) and personal mentors (www. disciplinementor.com). He is a frequent speaker and seminar leader at business, leadership and management conferences. His passion is to help people excel in their professional and personal life by helping them develop their self-discipline skills to combat the top issues: severe procrastination, poor time management, ineffective goal management, lack of focus, no sense of urgency and poor motivation. He also helps individuals improve their EQ skills (communication, relationship management, inter-personal, etc.) and leadership skills. He pioneered the *Discipline Mentoring Program* and *Professional/Personal Growth Program (P²GP)*. Mr. Kern is also the author of over 40 books.

Some of the titles include:

- DISCIPLINE: Six Steps to Unleashing Your Hidden Potential
- DISCIPLINE: Training the Mind to Manage Your Life
- DISCIPLINE: Mentoring Children for Success
- DISCIPLINE: Take Control of Your Life
- Going From Undisciplined to Self-Mastery: Five Simple Steps to Get You There
- Live Like You Are Dying: Making Your Life Count Moment by Moment

Mr. Kern is recognized as the foremost authority on practical guidance for solving management issues and challenges. He has devoted over 30 years helping professionals build competitive organizations. His client list reads like a who's who of American and international business. His client list includes Standard and Poor's, GE, The Weather Channel, News Corporation, Hong Kong Air Cargo Terminal (HACTL) and hundreds of other Fortune 500 and Global 2000 companies.

Mr. Kern is the founder and driving force behind the Enterprise Computing Institute (www.harriskern.com) and the best-selling series of books published by Prentice Hall. As founder of the Enterprise Computing Institute, he has brought together the industry's leading minds to publish how-to textbooks on the critical issues the IT industry faces. The series includes titles such as:

- IT Services
- CIO Wisdom
- CIO Wisdom II
- Managing IT as an Investment

Mr. Kern's goal is to arm individuals and organizations with the tools to empower them to become more productive and successful.

Additional Personal Information
More than Forty Years of Being Productive and Successful

Mr. Kern lives every day with a **sense of urgency**! Life is short and he makes use of every minute NOT hour or day! Mr. Kern pushes himself extremely hard (by choice):

- Exercises every day of the year
- Has traveled to every continent and hundreds of cities all over the world (some several times)
- Has established several successful businesses
- Purchased first home at the age of 19 in the San Francisco Bay Area
- Trained his mind and body to sleep four hours a night
- Financially set at the age of 38

Most people would consider his routine crazy and unhealthy; however, Mr. Kern is 60 years old and he has mastered the ultimate level of discipline since his early twenties. Mr. Kern believes that the body and mind should be pushed to the max every single day. The difference is he has the experience to do so; however, Mr. Kern would never push his clients in this manner unless, of course, this is their wish.

Mr. Kern's greatest assets are his caring demeanor, incomparable energy, and desire to help people manage their life efficiently. He wants to help as many people as possible fulfill their goals and aspirations.

My Contact Information
If you are still having difficulties holding yourself accountable, feel free to contact me to discuss your issues:
- Mobile: 818.404.9248
- Email: harris@harriskern.com.

I would prefer you call. I am a bit old-fashioned and prefer to hear your voice while you discuss your challenges with me. When it comes to dealing with sensitive issues, email is not always the proper vehicle to use.

Contact information for Leticia Gomez
If you are interested in writing and publishing a book, I strongly recommend that you get in touch with my longtime literary agent and close personal friend, Leticia Gomez. I have worked with many publishers/agents over the past two decades, and let me tell you, NO ONE is more sincere or has more integrity than Leticia Gomez of Savvy Literary Services. Most people in the publishing industry

are notorious for not having people-friendly skills. Sometimes it takes them days or even weeks to respond to an email. Their excuse is that they have too many books/clients to deal with. Nothing could be further from the truth. I worked with one of the top publishing houses in the world for over 10 years and the senior editor would oftentimes joke with me about how undisciplined he was and how unmotivated the organization was—no sense of urgency whatsoever! Leticia is the first person I have met (after publishing over 40 books) that is PASSIONATE about her work, RESPONSIVE to her clients and a PLEASURE to speak with. I love working with her!

She can be contacted at the following email address: savvyliterary@yahoo.com.

Special Message from the Author

At this stage of my life (elder years), I didn't have to write another book for the sake of adding onto my many accomplishments. My legacy has been solidified for a few decades now. I could just keep going to the gym every morning, which I will continue to do until the day I drop for good, manage my businesses (life coaching, organization performance and IT consulting), and write.

Writing a book is relentless and grueling work. I don't exactly consider it to be fun, but I am addicted to it. This particular book was extremely fulfilling because it was important for me to share my experiences to prevent a few workaholics from taking that deep plunge like I did. I wanted to help as many people as possible from destroying their lives. I sincerely hope I meet this objective.